The Senior Season

Celebrate Your Golden Years with

Reflection, Relevance, Revival…

Make the Rest of Your Life the Best of Your Life

❖

Robert Robotti

The Senior Season

Robert Robotti, Author

Rio Publications, affiliate of Journey Circle, LLC

San Diego, California

Copyright © 2018 by Robert Robotti

All rights reserved

Printed in the United States of America

ISBN-13 digit: 9781717870261

First Edition, 2018

For more information about The Senior Season call to action programs, including Journey Circle events and Family Legacy 2000, contact Robert Robotti at rrobotti@aol.com or visit our web site (www.TheSeniorSeason.com).

The Senior Season

~ *Acknowledgements* ~

To my wife, Marilyn, and my daughters, Tracy and Ashley, granddaughter Sadie, my mom, Josephine, in-laws Rose, Dan, Syl, Rochelle, Erin, and Theresa.

Special hugs for my long-time friends: Christiane, Larry, Marcus, Stefanie, Dolapo, Scott, Marc, Renee, Joe, Jeff, Cynthia, Rick, Janice, Aly, Kim, Dieter, Klaus, Lena, Buz, Steve, Butch, Gene, Nick, Kandace, Al, Kelli, Mark, Zepporah, Kathy, Keith, Carol, Cherie, Tal, Gigi, Matt, Eric, Don, and many new friends in San Diego, including my regular golf buddies: Richard, Ed, Emil, Bud, Chris, Neal, Jim, Kevin, Andy, Jack, Mark, and Wayne.

With appreciation to my author friends Mara Brown, Jan Moran, Tom Gay, and John Collins, for their kind input and mentorship and to Lauren Corallo, for her creative work on the cover, and to Charlie Seper of ebook Pioneers for his professional approach and presentation in formatting this book.

Also, a very special "thank you" and big hugs to Mary L. Holden for her professional editing, patience, and personal guidance. She really is an earth angel, who happened to become my editor for this book, and another guiding light on this journey.

A special acknowledgment to my good friend of over fifty years, Bill Rehm, for his constructive support in helping me get this book started.

Also, a note of appreciation to Wei Vivian He, CEO, ChinUSA Group Ltd; Associate Professor, Sichuan University; Doc, for translating this book for mainland China.

Thanks for bringing out the best in me.

~ Robert Robotti

The Senior Season

~ Endorsements ~

THE SENIOR SEASON *will give boomers insights to ideas and actions that are useful in addressing the complex issues facing our generation today. This book is an excellent gateway for self-exploration.*

~ Dolapo Asiru, Managing Partner, Hanover West

Your life journey in shifting your focus from 'success to significance' needs this book! Don't miss the opportunity to uncover the joy that finding your true significance can mean to you.

~ Tom Gay, CEO, Refer.Com

Does your age make you feel irrelevant? THE SENIOR SEASON *shows you how to live a life of relevance and to find happiness at any age.*

~ Jan Moran, Author, *The Winemakers*

This book is beneficial for people of all ages! As a young adult, I was encouraged by the refreshing take that you are never too old to follow your aspirations and live a successful and fulfilling life.

~ Sadie Radzin, Student

The Senior Season

Baby Boomers: This is a descriptive term for a person who was born between 1946 and 1964. The baby boomer generation makes up nearly 20% of the American public, or about 70 million people.

The Senior Season

Are you a baby boomer?

Then, this book is for, and about, you.

Use it as a valuable and enjoyable guide

on your path to become the better version of yourself.

This book is designed in a journal format for

readers who wish to write and preserve their reflections.

The Senior Season

You cannot do anything about the length of your life.

However, you can do something about its width and depth.

~ Evan Esar

The Senior Season

~ Contents ~

The Senior Season

In the end, it is not the years in your life that count.

It is the life in your years.

~ Abraham Lincoln

The Senior Season

~ Foreword ~

A number of years ago, I was introduced to Robert Robotti and I had the opportunity to spend many quality sessions with him in my role as his life coach. Our objective was to create a path for Robert to become the better version of himself. He has done just that. And he has supported and guided many others along the way. His road was not easily traversed; there were huge hurdles along the way. The primary obstacle that he had to overcome was the most important journey in his life: The one from his head to his heart. Here is how I described his journey in my book, *What Now…The Road from Success to Significance.*

> *"Robert opened up immediately during our early conversations and knew what direction he wanted to go…he wanted to develop a deeper aspect of himself. He had started his spiritual path years earlier with the study of Kabbalah, but he was now ready to move on to a broader consciousness; he wanted to find and develop his personal spirituality.*
>
> *One of the first things we did was to look at his life to help him find a more meaningful and deeper purpose. He was a very analytical man, which served him well in business, but it hindered him when exploring this new dimension of himself and his life. He came to discover that the more he learned about his true self, the more he wanted to learn and develop.*
>
> *We made huge progress together, although we did have our share of "resistance" conversations. But, the great thing about him was that he was open to try anything and willing to explore himself at a very deep level.*
>
> *When we talked about the idea of service in alignment with his purpose, he really took to that. So much so, that he realized that he wanted to use his resources and experience to gather a group of entrepreneurs and professionals in his home where people would be free to express the spiritual side of themselves. These gatherings*

would incorporate heartfelt topics like living in alignment with your purpose, the power of forgiveness, and the pursuit of meaning/fulfillment. These were topics that people may not otherwise have a place in their lives to talk about. We planned his dream and vision and invited dozens of people to meet at his home each month. This was the birth of "Journey Circle", a place where guests were invited to take off their masks and open their hearts. Robert started each evening with a statement that the primary hope and purpose of the event was that guests would have an 'aha' moment that would improve their lives. He then shared his personal experience on the chosen topic and then gently stepped back to allow guests to express themselves. In this format, the exchanges always grew into a vortex of energy during the event - and yes, there were many, many 'aha' moments.

These gatherings were magical for all in attendance, but especially for Robert. He found his purpose. It was: To provide an environment to encourage others to find their own 'aha' moments, personal growth, reflection, and deeper awareness, with fun, humor, love and relationship building. This perspective now carries into all aspects of his life - his family, his business, and his relationships.

Robert says that his life is now far richer, happier, and more fulfilled than he could have imagined. And his adventurous spirit, now ignited, will continue to grow, flourish, and expand. He is truly making a meaningful difference in his community and enjoys every minute of it. It fulfills and inspires him. He is truly living a life of significance, touching the lives of many others.

I am so proud of Robert for writing *The Senior Season*. I am certain that his wisdom, depth and life experiences can offer many seniors a new perspective on living more fulfilling lifestyles.

Let that be you. Find your purpose and let it start to shape and give meaning to your life - now - not later. Not when you are ill. Not when you find some time. Mine your purpose right now. Like a diamond that comes from coal, your purpose will be the rock that will sustain you. And it will carry you through every stage of your life. You will live your life on wings of light and joy! You will truly live a successful life of meaning and significance.

~ Mara Brown, Executive Life Coach, Author, Television Producer/Host

The Senior Season

Know that you are the perfect age. Each year is special and precious,

for you will only live it once. Be comfortable with growing older.

~ Louise Hay

The Senior Season

~ Introduction: Welcome to the Senior Season ~

There is nothing noble in being superior to your fellow man.

True nobility is being superior to your former self.

~ Ernest Hemingway

It is my hope that *The Senior Season* will offer you an opportunity to take a personal timeout, to reflect on your past, to consider your present choices, and to deepen your insights, as you prepare for a better future. Along the way, many of you will recognize that this time can be one of the most important adventures of your life: The journey from your head to your heart. It's the pathway from thinking, to feeling, and thinking again…and then choosing the best path forward.

Throughout this book, you are invited to pause and reflect on your own treasured journey. The space after each question offers an opportunity to write out your reflections, and intentions, as you define your perspectives, behaviors, and choices on how you want to relate to people and things in your life: the "who and how" you want to be. Your answers may stimulate new and quality choices that can lead you to living a life of good and service, in your golden years.

As you respond to the questions, enjoy the process as a walk down memory lane with yourself. You are a private audience of *one*. Answer only those questions that will serve you best. You will uncover *aha! moments* by engaging in this manner, and you can begin the powerful process of designing your plan for the future. Be genuine. Be vulnerable. Be courageous.

If you want to preserve your reflections, use this book as a personal journal and preserve it in a place for review in the months and years ahead.

If you wish to share this journey with someone you care about, you are setting the stage for a more intimate and authentic connection with them, while fostering mutual empathy, trust, and understanding.

Be assured that you will gain valuable insight from reflecting on these questions. I have done so and gained a broadened perspective that has enabled me to create positive change in my life.

You are invited to start your own journey of self–discovery with your thoughtful answer to the initial question on the next page. Just think, and feel, and think again....

The Senior Season - a Journey of Self-Discovery

The key to wisdom is to know all the right questions.

~ John Simone

- *What are you grateful for?*

- *Where are you living right now? The past, present, or future?*

- *Do you want to be the best version of yourself? How can you do it?*

- *Do you have a clear purpose in life? What is it? What can it become?*

- *What are the most important things to you in life? Why?*

- *How can you make your life more meaningful?*

- *What are your main gifts, tools, skill sets?*

- *How can you be a good role model and messenger as a senior?*

- *How can you enhance your relationships with family?*

- *Do you have a plan for the rest of your life? If not, are you ready to design one?*

- *Are you ready to write your own book, or memoir? What would be your book's title?*

- *What things do you need to do to feel relevant in your senior years?*

- *Do you have a bucket list of things to do, places to see?*

- *Are you ready to make an 'inside' bucket list of how to feel, and who to be?*

~ Chapter 1 ~
A Time to Ponder Your Priorities

"What lies behind us and what lies before us are tiny matters compared to what lies within us."

~ Ralph Waldo Emerson

I am 71 years old. There, I said it! That's hard for me to believe, let alone say. Like many others, I look into the mirror some days and wonder: "How did I get here? What's my journey all about, and why?" And then, the obvious questions: "Where am I headed?" and "Do I need a plan?"

Do you feel the same? Does time seem to go by so quickly that you rarely allow yourself enough space to reflect on your own journey, let alone make a plan for the future?

Some people say, "live in the present, live in the now," and I understand that. But the fact is that your past choices and experiences offer a valuable window on how you arrived at this moment and place in time. It is important to understand and re-evaluate your personal beliefs, perceptions, and tendencies, and to be mindful of where shifts may be beneficial to you. The choices that you make now, in designing a fresh, life-style plan will define the quality of life in *your* senior season.

For me, I feel that *now* is the right time to pause and reflect, to set a quality tone for this unique phase of my life. It's time for me to identify clear markers and a solid foundation for my future. Like you, I can say that my life has been an exciting journey. It has served up a paradox of events, connected by light and dark threads, all intimately mingled. I have experienced a broad variety of challenges and choices that have somehow blended together and delivered me to this very special time and place in my life. So how will my new path unfold? How can I live a fulfilling life in *my* senior season? I needed to go deep and made a big decision, and voila! A plan came together.

Perhaps you know the old adage: *You teach best what you need to learn.* The purpose of this book is exactly that for me; I want to learn how to live a life of significance in my senior season.

To realize this lofty vision, I needed to identify and embrace my priorities. I needed a new life strategy. I took a "timeout." I reflected on the past, I evaluated my present choices, and I deepened my insights. I have since made a life plan that I will share with you in this book. My plan goes beyond what I choose *to do*; it is about who I choose *to be* along the way. I believe the latter choice allows me to move closer to a journey of happiness and fulfillment for the rest of my life! I hope that this book inspires you to create a life plan of your own.

The following questions are meant to touch your inner spirit. Ponder them carefully. Take a deep breath, close your eyes, and reflect. Your answers can help you prepare a rewarding path for your future. Remember, this is all about you. Enjoy the ride!

People who control their inner experience are better able to

determine the quality of their lives, which is as close

as any of us can come to being happy.

~ Anonymous

Reflections on Your Life and Times

Who are the most important people to you in life? Why?

What are the most important things to you in life? Why?

What are you passionate about? Why?

What character traits you are most proud of? Why?

How can you describe your values? What do you represent?

Are you ready to re-evaluate any of your beliefs or behaviors?

What are the biggest actions you can take to create the biggest results in your life?

Gandhi said, "My life is my message." What is your life message?

"You cannot control what happens to you, but you can control your attitude toward what happens to you, and in that, you will be mastering change rather than allowing it to master you." This wisdom is from Sri Ram. Does this apply to you? How?

The mystery of human existence lies not in just staying alive,

but in finding something to live for.

~ Fyodor Dostoyevsky

~ Chapter 2 ~
The Times, They Are A-Changin'

When you change the way you look at things, the things you look at change.

~ Wayne Dyer

In pondering a plan for my senior season, I wondered if my voice, and perhaps our collective voices as seniors, is not as relevant as it once was, or as it can be.

Why is that?

Perhaps, many seniors who have moved on from their careers and accomplishments remain emotionally invested in those aspects of the past. They feel that the rest of the world seems to march to the beat of a different drummer. For some, there is a certain stress caused by the lessening or elimination of an important role they played, which can lead to a loss of self-esteem, and anxiety.

In addition, the role that seniors have in their families evolves. Parents and elder relatives require caretaking as they age. Spouses may uncouple. Children grow up, leave home, and perhaps reside far away. Advancing age itself leads to the loss of friends through illness and death. Grief, the loss of anything that once seemed constant—is its own brand of anxiety. These changes often cause a sense of isolation. Add these conditions to the weight of leaving the work force, declining health, and changing relationships to understand why many people with at least six decades of life under their belts feel lost and voiceless.

Many seniors may also feel trivialized by the fast advances in information technology that younger generations absorb with ease. This gap has added new intellectual and emotional hurdles for seniors to navigate that never existed before. Social media platforms and apps can act as potent change agents in many seniors' lives with just a flick of a finger or a voice command, yet seniors shy away from these advances rather than inquire, learn, and interact with the many platforms available to them. These elders then miss out on golden opportunities to express their opinions, relate with others, and they ultimately lose a sense of being relevant.

Have you observed that some seniors seem to give up? They feel that their personal story has diminished, and with that, a sense of lack, weakness, and loneliness rolls in like fog. Their entire life's purpose seems to have become narrow and out of focus, others seem to live in the past and become less active. They spend more time at home, oftentimes alone. They find less and less reason to socialize and communicate outside their family. They may focus on concerns about health for themselves, their spouse, pets, family members and friends, to a point of losing their own spirit. Many did not prepare well financially for this time of life and do not know where or how they will live out their final years. They slowly but surely feel less relevant, almost purposely. Meanwhile, the uncertainty of the future looms in the foreground. These familiar challenges for seniors are not new.

My dad brought this to mind for me, many years ago. I will always remember the many times I asked him, during his retirement, what he had been doing all day. Too often, his answer was, "Just killing time." That was exactly what he was doing. He had so much more to offer; but his life, in his own eyes, became less and less valued.

Are you tempted to "just kill time?" If so, I want you to know that there is another side to this story for today's seniors. This is a *good time* to be a Baby Boomer.

Have you recognized that Boomers (born; 1946-1964) are the most significant senior group of all time? In the United States alone, there are over 70 million of us, a bit over 20 percent of the U.S. population. It is a fact that Boomers have observed, experienced, and accomplished much more than every previous generation. We are the wealthiest, most physically fit, intellectually advanced and the most driven to consume.

We, the Boomers, have already had a tremendous impact on every aspect of life today. Within our age cohort, our peers have created a legacy that seems to have begun in earnest with Rock 'n Roll, Beatlemania, Woodstock, and man's first walk on the moon. We have broken barriers in racial and gender equality, cultural diversity, music, cinema, education, politics, finance, food, technology, and environmental protection. We have been at the forefront of many of history's greatest advances in medicine, manufacturing, science, the arts, communication, transportation and more. Since the turn of the 21st century, we've supported and participated in fascinating accomplishments in robotics, artificial intelligence, synthetic biology, 3D printing, GPS, and thousands of computer applications.

What seems to be overlooked, however, is that many of us still have an incredible amount of *firepower*. We have tremendous skills, experience, resources, and a love for life. We are blessed to live in the greatest senior generation of all time. Today, we have more time, more toys, more choices, and more opportunities than any senior group in history. Yet, the challenge is to combine these advantages with quality personal choices so that we can truly experience our golden years to the fullest.

We seniors need to be challenged. There is no benefit to becoming stale, stagnant, and irrelevant. We need to pause and contemplate the direction and priorities in our lives. We need to create a personal philosophy for a better tomorrow.

We've been successful as adults, now, let's be significant as seniors. As retirees, let us reshape the way aging itself is perceived. We can be the role models and messengers for the generations that will follow us. Where do we begin?

Let's re-discover ourselves. Then, let's each make a plan! A good way to start is by asking yourself some intimate questions.

Self-Reflection: Your Senior Season

What advice would you give yourself three years ago to better prepare for today?

1.

2.

3.

4.

Do you have a life plan for the next three, or 10 years? If not, are you ready to design one?

If you have only one year to live, what would you do?

1.

2.

3.

4.

What are the physical expectations you see for yourself as you age?

What are the emotional expectations you see for yourself as you age?

What are the spiritual expectations you see for yourself as you age?

What does your family expect from you as you age?

What do you need to accept now that is different as a senior?

What aspects of your life can you enhance or change to benefit those around you?

How can you bring value, joy, and peace to each day?

What can you do to care for and maintain your health and fitness?

How can you use your gifts, your skills, and your blessings to help others?

How do you balance your perspective in life between your head and your heart?

How and where can you find new motivation for engaging in work and play that sustains your soul, and keeps your outlook on the positive side?

How can you make your life more meaningful, starting today?

What drives you? When are you most inspired, most motivated, most charged up?

What do you do during those times? How can you do more, starting today?

How can you change someone's life for the better?

Who are the five people you spend the most time with? Are these people sharing joy with you, enabling you, or holding you back?

1.

2.

3.

4.

5.

Who can you move into your inner circle to enhance your awareness, interests, happiness, and lifestyle?

What's the top priority in your life right now? What are you doing about it?

Do you want to leave a legacy, and if so, what do you want it to be?

The purpose of life is to contribute in some way to making things better.

~ Robert F. Kennedy

~ Chapter 3 ~
My Senior Plan

There are two fatal errors that keep great things from coming to life:

1. Not finishing   2. Not starting

~ Anonymous

At this stage of life, I feel blessed about many things. Thankfully, I have good health. I have a wonderful family, quality friends, and incredible memories.

Even with such blessings though, I do struggle at times. Once I retired, I felt like I crossed an imaginary line. I moved away from my familiar and exhilarating arena of work, play, and teammates (my tribe) to a new place in time that has few signposts, and a much narrower path. I had always thought of retirement as a goal, in and of itself.

It is not. I have to admit, I was not prepared. I had no plan. I felt like a peaceful warrior without a battlefield.

Initially, I assumed, like many retirees, that I would simply find a way to keep *busy… but busy doing what*? That is an ongoing issue for most seniors…and it is the true focal point of this book, and for me. I have since pledged to myself to design a plan for being busy in a way that brings out the best in me.

Today's seniors have many choices to consider if they want to live an active life style. After all, they have better circumstances and choices than those who lived in prior generations. Year after year, people live longer, are better educated, and have access to more leisurely activities, interests, hobbies and the superhighway of social technology. Even with these advantages and abundant choices, most seniors are not fulfilled; they lose themselves in wandering around, day after day, seemingly without a clear, and meaningful agenda. They have not really thought things out. They have not planned ahead. Their sense of relevancy is diminishing.

Society hasn't properly addressed the issue, either. Fragments of information are available in publications and online, but there is no definitive guide on this very personal and life shifting topic. There is certainly no cookie cutter approach for a "senior plan."

In my case, I recognized that I needed to create a personalized plan, but had to ask, "Where and how should I start?" I knew that the foundation of my plan needed to be filtered through the many life lessons I was blessed to experience, blended with the information that I could access through online research, and one to one discussions with my peers. I recognized that I had to turn on my learning switch. Do the research. Observe. Dig deep into myself. Be creative, in looking for answers. Ask for help. Walk the walk!

As I embarked on this journey, some interesting thoughts arose, adding new layers of questions. I realized that I needed to invest genuine time and effort into a plan for my senior season. I deserved it. I needed to make a commitment to the success of my future, in a different way than I ever imagined. If I was going to be busy, as a senior, I wanted to do it as a *human being*, instead of a *human doing*. I was ready to make a plan.

Where would I start?

To begin with, I acknowledged that I am somewhat analytical. So, *cross-examining* myself seemed like a good way to initiate the process. I knew that intimate questions needed to be addressed, preferably with written answers, so that I could really absorb and review the entirety of my reflections. I started with questions like *"Who am I, to me? Who am I, to others? In what direction do I want to lead my life? What makes me happy? What makes me feel fulfilled? What do I want to be, do and feel?"*

My answers to these initial questions added more and more dimension to my evolving plan. Layer by layer, my newly formed perspective led me on a path of self-awareness. By taking a timeout to question myself, from both an inner and outer perspective, my answers became a gateway of fresh thoughts and feelings, allowing me to re-define the blueprint for my present, and my future.

I eventually called this blueprint my "Internal Bucket List" and I propose that you design your own plan, using this book as your personal journal. The list includes many of the things that one wants to do, feel, and be, from the inside out. In a sense, the list is actually about who you are, what roles you choose to play, and how to be a better senior citizen. The purpose is to make life more meaningful by connecting you to things larger than yourself, such as self-awareness, love, compassion, gratitude, humility, and a range of other joy filled emotions.

On the next page is my Internal Bucket List

Does it align with some of your core choices?

I want to raise my self-awareness. I want to make wiser choices.

I want to have genuine meaning and purpose in my everyday life.

I want to live with joy, peace, happiness, and contentment.

I want to live with love, passion, compassion, and forgiveness.

I want to embrace personal growth, creativity, and positive change.

I want to express my gratitude for my blessings, every day.

I do not want to fade into the sunset.

I want to be active. I want to be more than an observer in the game of life.

I do not want to be busy doing trivial things.

I want to make a difference.

I want to enjoy my time while sharing, helping, guiding, and inspiring others.

I want to pay it forward, by being kind towards others.

I want to engage in rewarding, new experiences.

I want to be the best me that I was meant to be.

I want to always be relevant.

Being a senior is a wonderful time for change. A time to become content with *who* one is, while still being an active contributor to the planet. I now realize that at the top of my inner bucket list is my new focus and journey: *to become the better version of myself*.

Reflections on Your Senior Plan

The following questions are offered to help you prepare your own senior plan. Your answers can lead towards identifying your purpose, values, goals, personal strengths, blind spots, and action plans to live your best life.

Do you spend your time and energy feeling and doing the things that you love? Are you sleepwalking through life?

Start your senior plan by listing five things that make you happy.

1.

2.

3.

4.

5.

In what quality ways can you be active and relevant?

1.

2.

3.

How can you be more creative and productive?

1.

2.

3.

How can you best continue to learn, grow, and mentor?

1.

2.

3.

How can you raise awareness and gain control of your emotional status?

1.

2.

3.

You want to make continued efforts to get and stay healthy. What is your plan?

1.

2.

3.

What resources can you offer to help your family, friends, and community?

1.

2.

3.

How can you show your gratitude and demonstrate a good attitude?

1.

2.

3.

How can you feel in tune with your best self, more often?

1.

2.

3.

Why can reflecting more on your past, present and future, help you design a better future?

How do you resist temptation to judge yourself and others in unfair or harsh ways?

Do you want to feel closer to your family?

   Here's what you can change and do.

1.

2.

3.

Do you want to feel closer to your friends?

   Here's what you can change and do.

1.

2.

3.

Do you want to feel closer to your faith?

   Here's what you can change and do.

1.

2.

3.

Do you feel great when you allow yourself to feel wonder and enthusiasm for life?

Here's how you can act and think with that kind of grace, ease, and joy.

1.

2.

3.

Do you want to be the best version of yourself?

How you can do it?

1.

2.

3.

Notes:

Getting old is like climbing a mountain: you get a little out of breath,

but the view is much better!

~ Ingrid Bergman

~ *Chapter 4* ~
Finding the Light

Empower yourself not as a victim of circumstances
but as the source of your own experience. The whole game changes when
you realize the answer is within you.

~ Alan Cohen

My life's timeline first encountered semi-retirement when I was 57 years old. During that time, I found an important piece of life's puzzle. Some may call it *finding the light*, but I recognized it as finding my *spirituality*. Many folks in the Baby Boom generation are not comfortable with the term or the concepts behind it. Many, like me, were raised in a designated religious affiliation, and we rarely discussed our own thoughts and beliefs. I feel very fortunate that I was introduced to spiritualty as a life style choice. I embraced it, and the difference in my approach to life is breathtaking.

Spirituality is not a religion; it has no dogma, no rules, no *my way or the highway* approach. It is about reaching deep within and being the *better version of yourself*, out of a genuine choice, as a citizen of the world. It is about expressing and experiencing those aspects of yourself that genuinely feel good—your thoughts, perceptions, behavior, and beliefs; the things you hold dearest. Spirituality's path leads you to discover that the key to the *Kingdom of Heaven* is actually in your own heart. You just need to take the longest journey in life—the one from *your head to your heart*—to find the key and unlock your soul.

I have to admit that it took me about six months, even after I became an avid student of spirituality, to begin to understand what my own humanity was all about. Once I absorbed the key principles of everyman's spirituality, I accepted that this was actually a life style choice and I engaged in the process. I pledged to embrace life, albeit in a different way than ever before. I learned new ways to communicate, to create, to grow, and to challenge myself. I promised inwardly that I would not fall into a way of thinking and acting based on lack. Instead, I promised myself I would focus on abundance. The transition to deeper self-awareness has been quite a journey, and it constantly evolves in many ways, as it should.

The gateway to my transformation came from unexpected sources. In a very short time, I was able to get off the express train pursuing success and fancy toys and instead, I engaged in the realm of self-reflection, to discover a better vision of myself.

The beginning of this new journey and my senior season really began one week in 2003, a time I will never forget. It was one of the major turning points in my life. My financial advisor said, "Bob, after you close this big deal, you will be at a point where you can think about retiring and really enjoy life."

That comment threw me off guard. "Retire? How would that work?" I wondered aloud, "I'm in my mid-50s, I have so much energy and I love what I am doing, why would I retire, what else would I do? Hmm." Before that moment, I'd never thought of what I would do with a lot of free time. I had no plan.

I wasn't about to retire, but I did hear the wake-up call. I began to evaluate where I stood in my story; past, present and future. I realized that my advisor was right. I had achieved enough financial success that I could at least semi-retire, but I had no plans to do so. The larger reality though, was the realization that I had not taken time to slow down, to get out of the rat race long enough to even think about who I was, as a person. It was time to take a break. A personal *time out* was in order.

As my mind wandered during the next few days, a strong voice inside me became louder. It said, "Is that all there is? You worked so hard all these years and now you have 'made it.' Yes, you have met your goals on many levels and earned the right to retire. But look into yourself, what will you do now? Just continue working hard and earning more? How does that make sense? You know that you have so much more to offer, to discover."

This was my turning point. Yes, I was living a good life. I enjoyed excellent health, owned a penthouse condo, had all the toys, bells and whistles, was CEO of a great company (one of top 500 companies in U.S. according to *Inc.* magazine), enjoyed good family relationships, wonderful partners and a diverse group of quality friends; even had a golf hole-in-one that year; and, life as a contented bachelor on top of it all. "What could possibly be wrong with this picture?" I thought. But I knew then and there, that *something* was definitely missing.

It was *me*!

I did not know whom, or what, to turn to for advice on this highly sensitive revelation. It seemed like such a paradox; "How could I be on top of the world and feel somewhat lost, at the same time?" I decided that I would ask one of my good friends, a jetsetter, yet a person I considered to have her feet on the ground. She exhibited great character. "How have you managed your success?" I asked her when we next met.

She simply said, "Spirituality."

I thought, "Great one word answer, but what does that mean?"

She went on to say, "You embrace 'spirituality' when you recognize that the universe is bigger than your personal story. Once you genuinely accept this, you can take off your mask and open your heart to wonderful things, like grateful living, compassion, forgiveness and love."

I was stunned to hear this. She may have been one of the last people I would have expected to learn this life altering commentary from. The previous week I was watching her make a $1,000 bet on a blackjack hand in Las Vegas! She *must* have known something that I needed to know because she had it all together. I now, more than ever, appreciate who she is on the *inside* as well as on the *outside*.

I said, "OK. That sounds like something that can make a difference. How do I start?"

She told me that *Kabbalah* might be a good starting point. Kabbalah is a term for a type of ancient wisdom; it means *to receive*. It is an esoteric method, discipline, and school of thought about how the universe and life works, and how humans may gain fulfillment. It originated centuries ago in Judaism, but is not a religion.

My friend suggested that I attend an orientation class in Los Angeles to see if it might strike a chord with me. I agreed and decided to learn more. With gratitude, I hugged my friend and left the restaurant. My new journey began.

As fate would have it, I decided to have my car washed on the way back to the office, not anticipating that a fundamental change in my life was about to happen. As I was waiting in line to pay the cashier, I noticed a rack of books. On the lower shelf, one odd book title immediately got my attention. The title of the book was *The Power of Kabbalah*. I had to sound out "kab-bal-ah" to even be sure that it was the same word that I heard earlier in the day from my friend. Of course, it was the same. It was meant to be.

The next week, I was sitting in an orientation class in the Kabbalah Center in Los Angeles. Marcus, the instructor, was filled with energy and enthusiasm. I listened attentively and I had an *aha!* moment within the first 40 minutes of the workshop. "This is it! This is the new direction for me!" I exclaimed inwardly. I felt like everything that I was now seeking rose up in me during that first hour. I felt excited, happy, filled with new promise and purpose. I was hit with a new awareness of humanity's greatest callings: hope, gratitude, compassion, forgiveness, and love.

I wanted more. This was my turning point, I thought.

This is also when my *higher self* was awakened. I didn't even know I had a higher self, waiting to surface in my consciousness. However, this internal voice was clear and inspiring, I felt its' guidance in a powerful message; "I am your true self. I want to be heard…and seen. Let's do this!"

I immediately felt the strong connection to my inner spirit - I gave it a name: "Rio", the Spanish word for *river*. I imagined a serene river flowing gently in a beautiful scenic vista; the name and vision came to me naturally, and felt so right.

I soon registered for two courses and during the next several weeks of study, I was enlightened and guided on a new path, as I rediscovered and emotionally felt my genuine humanity. I sought out new people to help and engage with in my new approach to understand and accept the premise that we are all brothers and sisters. There is no dogma in Kabbalah; it is simply: "Take what you want and leave the rest behind." I loved the sense of freedom and exploration to discover my own path, to be all I could be.

I began looking at the world quite differently--not to take, but to give. Not to just think, but to feel. Not to do, but to be. And there was more—it was about letting go of doubt, uncertainty, and fear. It felt so good. Kabbalah called all of the good things in life the *light*, and I wanted as much light as I could get.

One day, soon after my initial Kabbalah classes, I sat in my office and I could feel that things were different for me. Most of our staff could sense that something changed in me too. I was floating on air.

"But," I wondered; "could I experience and express myself as 'Rio' - my kindly, higher self - in the office, and still manage to be as effective as I was during my ten-year term as CEO of my large and growing company?

"Yes," was my next thought, "I can and I will."

At first, I tried combining the two sides of *me* into one, but it was not quite working. I decided to keep my two profiles somewhat separated, with as much overlap as possible.

That worked better.

I spoke to my partner, Mark, and expressed my newfound vision. I told him I needed to take off a week a month, as a personal retreat, for my spiritual growth. He kindly agreed.

To be fair, I offered to take a 25 percent cut in executive pay, but it was worth it. My ideal spirituality week pulled me out of the proverbial rat race and onto a path where I felt fulfilled by being more kind, considerate, charitable, caring, sharing, and loving, than I had ever been. During these times, I stood up inside myself as *Rio*, seeking to be all I could be, from the inside out. I would not engage in thoughts of uncertainty, doubt, fear, and scarcity. Instead, during my retreat weeks, I would focus on self-awareness, compassion, gratitude, and humanity.

This was an amazing process that worked really well for me, right from the beginning. When I returned to the office at the end of a retreat week, I was fresh. It was like someone hit a reset button. My decision-making ability was crisp and wiser. My interaction with staff and investor clients was dynamic and gentle at the same time. I was placing myself in the other person's position, observing my own exchanges from multiple perspectives. Things just seemed to flow easily.

My 'spirituality weeks' were among the best times in my adult life. I attended many Kabbalah classes and read dozens of non-Kabbalah related spiritually oriented books for the first time. Among my favorites were these books: *Conversations with God*, by Neale Donald Walsch (the entire series); *A Deep Breath of Life,* by Alan Cohen (a daily book of inspiration that I have been reading now for 14 years); books by the Dalai Lama on purpose and happiness; *The Biography of a Yogi*, by Paramahansa Yogananda; *The Secret*, by Rhonda Byrne; and, many, many more. I also listened to many inspirational audiobooks by Deepak Chopra, Maryann Williamson, Andrew Weil, M.D., and Wayne Dyer. I read books about spirituality, breathing and breath work, yoga, meditation. I even read *Spirituality for Dummies*! I was hooked, and felt really good about it.

During this time, a memorable story unfolded when I agreed to meet a business client for a large, commercial real estate opportunity, in Florida, that came up during one of my retreat weeks, it was an important meeting for the company, and I decided to go. I went into the meeting totally in the persona of Rio. I was so calm and peaceful that I got the deal without asking for it. We did not even talk much business. For the greater part of the meeting, we discussed humanity and kindness. It turned out to be the most profitable deals that I had ever done.

After a few months of living this seemingly dual identity—one week focused on living *on* life (the Rio me)—three weeks focused on living *in* life (the impatient, aggressive, competitive, business first, ego personality in me), I recognized that I began to have a dual perspective of my life path. One life was as Rio, and the other was the ego self.

Of course, I wanted to do well and succeed in business, and I knew my company needed strong leadership, but I also wanted to embrace and enhance everyone in my circle of influence. I wanted all of us to be conscious of the wonderful world around us and to feel free to express and experience ourselves in that manner.

We are not human beings having a spiritual experience.

We are spiritual beings having a human experience.

~ Pierre Teilhard de Chardin

Reflections on Your Aha! Moments

Remember, and write some aha! moments you had during childhood and your teen years.

Remember, and write some aha! moments you had as a young adult.

Remember, and write some aha! moments you had as a spouse.

Remember, and write some aha! moments you had as a parent.

Remember, and write some aha! moments you had as a student.

Remember, and write some aha! moments you had in your career.

Remember, and write some aha! moments you had in the military.

Remember, and write some aha! moments you had as an adult.

Remember, and write some aha! moments you had as a senior.

Remember, and write some aha! moments you had at any other time in your life.

~ *Chapter 5* ~
How Can Your 'Higher Self' Serve You?

Your higher self is always nudging you toward
a resolution of the conflicts that you experience in your life,
so that you will have room for serenity and harmony.

~ Wayne Dyer

As you can see from my turning point in identifying the 'Rio' in me, one way to break the bonds of habitual behavior is to identify and embrace those parts of yourself that you like the most, your *higher self.*

Many adults are uncomfortable in consistently expressing and experiencing the more authentic, kinder, gentler, peaceful sides of themselves. Instead, they may live the kind of life required of a competitively charged environment, a consistently negative news cycle, a broad variety of complex, dramatic relationships, and other daily doses of uncertainty, doubt, and fear.

Many people get caught up in the swirl of life's challenges and multiple story lines that weave their way through daily life and the lives of others we know and, as a result, we feel compelled to make emotional adjustments, judgments, and immediate decisions, that are not to our benefit. Have you felt the domino effect of living this way?

There is a better way to live. You can take control by forming sound spiritual, psychological, and emotional foundations to position yourself in the best possible manner, as you navigate each day's events. When you intuitively know what makes you feel happy, content, and full of life, you understand what thoughts and choices are needed to get you there. You develop a finely tuned internal "call to action" that guides you in a positive and fulfilling way.

Many refer to this intuitive, natural state as the *higher self.* Some may refer to it as an *alter ego*. The *alter ego* is apart from the *ego*, and can be defined as that part of your being that is more authentic than the ego. This higher self, if embraced, will be your true self; the you who is ready, willing, and able to consistently choose a path to achieve the vision of a better life purpose.

The *higher self* is your true essence. It emerges when you can identify the ego and shut it down, leaving the authentic you to shine; the one deep down inside yourself with no labels, no tainted beliefs, or social masks. It is the intuitive you, the *you* that knows your very existence is what makes you amazing, beautiful, valuable, and divine. From that point on, it is a matter of reframing your approach to everything. You realize that you have an inner light that guides your way. You know that your inner peace and happiness do not depend on external influences. You can feel your connection to the universe, to all of humanity, as your brothers and sisters. You can live your natural dream of celebrating life in a peaceful, joyous, loving, and compassionate way.

On the other hand, the ego persona can be thought of as the mask you put on to face the world. It is all about the different roles you play with your image, in your own story. The ego is easily seen in others but difficult to recognize in yourself. All too often, you become aware that the ego is on stage and performing live. The ego inflates through favorable comparisons against others, by persistence in winning (sometimes, at all costs), in owning possessions, and it especially shows itself as exaggerated pride. It deflates when confronted with jealousy, blame, gossip, anxiety, fear, self-criticism, and disingenuous attitudes.

To be fair, it is incredibly challenging to dismiss the allure of the ego and be led by your higher self. When you manage to tap into this deeper part of *you* even for a few minutes a day, your life will improve in many magical and beautiful ways. This is because even a droplet worth of love, wisdom, or courage coming from your higher self is a thousand times more powerful than a negative message coming from the ego.

A good question may be "As a senior why would you want an alter ego"? The answer is that identifying an alter ego can help you in many ways, most importantly, to encourage you to act and feel as your true self. Here is a story about how my *higher self* served me in a life changing way:

About three months after I began my spiritual studies, and during one of my retreat weeks, I was set up on a blind date, at a golf course by a mutual friend. It was then that I met a beautiful and sweet woman, Marilyn. She was suffering through one of the toughest times in her life. She was battling for custody of her 4-year-old daughter during a bitter divorce battle.

Marilyn and I enjoyed playing golf with-each other that day and we agreed to have a follow-up to our blind date. Later that week, on a Friday night, I arrived at Marilyn's apartment and was greeted by her daughter, Ashley, a very pretty, and charming little girl. Ashley and I bonded over some fun gifts that I brought for her to play with, and I joined her on the floor as she opened them. It was the beginning of a wonderful, new relationship.

Marilyn and I then went out to dinner and had one of the most difficult and stressful first date experiences imaginable. She talked exclusively about her divorce, and her custody battle for her daughter. Although my ego was attracted to Marilyn, I wanted to call it an early night. However, the Rio in me was present, as my higher self. Rio guided me to ask Marilyn for more and more information, about the status of the divorce case, and the impact on Marilyn, and Ashley. I found myself asking how I could help, in any way. Against my ego's better judgment, the Rio in me asked Marilyn for another date the following Sunday. That date was the stepping-stone to our marriage, nine months later!

I am fortunate that I made the choice to pursue that relationship. I definitely would not have done so if Rio had not surfaced three months earlier. My ego would not have been willing to express and experience the compassion that ignited our relationship. I can honestly say the relationships I have with Marilyn and Ashley to this day are the best things that have happened to me since my daughter, Tracy, and granddaughter, Sadie came into my life.

Marilyn and Ashley have helped me to learn and grow, and to become more of a whole person. I continue to look forward to a great journey with my entire family going forward. They all literally bring out the best in me. *Thank you, Rio, for setting me on this path!*

Have you identified your own alter ego, your higher self? Maybe as an entrepreneur, a professional, a dedicated worker, a parent and/or a spouse, you found that you were always busy meeting the challenges of operating and managing a career commitment, and a family. Perhaps you felt that spending time alone, relaxing, and *just being* was not the best use of your time. Even the idea of taking a time out to allow a reset of your energy was somehow not appropriate, or right. Therefore, you buried those aspects of yourself so deep that you forgot they were there and you remained busy doing things, pursuing success, or just muddling through, and now, you find yourself doing similar things 10, 20, and even 30 years later. If so, this is now a good time to stand up inside yourself and make the changes that you know you want, because they can benefit you.

One of the great things about being a senior is that you can *just be* and people will understand. The question is, "Can *you* just be?"

The higher awareness that I have discovered has helped to make me become a better version of myself by allowing me space to create a positive environment and perspective. It also enables me to feel that I have a way to deal with any adversity, from a heart centered approach, rather than an external approach. I have become a strong advocate of "It's not so much 'what' happens to you as much as 'how' you react to what happens, that matters." This approach describes situations where we can call on the Rio side of our nature, to make things easier and better for all parties involved.

Are you in touch with your higher self? *Take some time to contemplate this question!*

I want to end this chapter with a final message about the alter ego. What is your alter ego, really? So many people seem to have difficulty understanding it in relationship to the ego. The Latin meaning of alter ego is other self—usually created to live out another version of the self. The words in Latin are said to have been used often by Cicero in referring to "a second self, a trusted friend."

There are many fictional examples of people who have had famous alter egos, and make for interesting reading. Today's versions might include references to cartoon and book characters, like Bruce Wayne as Batman, Peter Parker as Spiderman and Clark Kent as Superman...even the famous Jekyll and Hyde character in that classic novel by Robert Louis Stevenson.

In real life, however, everyone can acknowledge the times their alter ego has guided them to an alternative view of their world. It empowers you. It guides you. It inspires you. It may manifest itself as a hidden character trait in you that shines in courage. It may be your inner voice that guides you to embrace your soul instead of the rat race—even for a few moments at a time. And it is your sense of intuition to make a choice that may not seem practical, but feels right. For some, you may find it easier to access your alter ego when you allow yourself to chill a bit, to mellow out and when you actually smell the roses and express gratitude for life's blessings. For others, it may take a rude awakening, something that shakes your foundation; but either way, your alter ego is your life's muse. Use it wisely, and often.

For the balance of this book, the terms *alter ego* and *higher self* are used interchangeably.

Reflections on Your Higher Self...

How can you connect with your higher self? Take off your social mask and leave your ego at the door. Live in your higher consciousness. Be your authentic self. Open your heart. Dig deep. Learn who you are. Decide who you want to be. Go with your intuition. Trust your inner voice to guide you.

Do you feel that you have an alter ego?

Is it your higher self, or something else?

Would you consider using a name to identify your higher self to distinguish it from your ego, and your lesser self?

What name would you choose? Why?

From your higher self-perspective, can you see past choices that you would have made differently?

Can you see possible future choices that you might make differently from this viewpoint?

What benefits can you gain in life by making these shifts?

How can you enhance your role within your family?

Reflect on all of your key family relationships. Define the current overall level of respect, love, and behavior.

How can you enhance your friendships?

Remember, a true friend is someone who knows everything about you, but still loves you, and, visa versa. Can you commit to offering strong emotional support to friends?

Can you make your friends aware that you want to be the "wind beneath their wings?"

How do you define yourself in community? An excellent way to do this is to accept people as they are, faults and all. Recognize the good in others. Go out of your comfort zone to help someone. Just say 'hello' or smile to people you pass. Give gratitude to people who offer you goods and services. Offer good deeds, thoughts, and service in return.

How can you enhance your role in community?

How can you feel closer to God? Many find the most direct way to feel closer to their God, is to simply give gratitude for the amazing miracle of life, every morning when you wake, and every evening as you are about to sleep. Everything will flow from there. Is this true for you?

Do you feel that you have your own connectedness with God? Describe the connection.

Think about a day that you consider perfect. Sometimes, it is the simplest of things, like taking a "blessed interruption" to smell the roses, or just spending time in nature, or writing your memoirs, or sending warm letters to people you care about. Any of these things can make you feel connected to the universe.

What are your connectors?

What does a perfect day look like to you?

How can you take better care of yourself, including physical, emotional, mental and spiritual wellness?

How can you improve your diet, exercise, energy, flexibility, breathing, grooming, manage illness, sleep, release stress, feel peace and joy, feel more alive, enjoy relationships, hobbies and chores, be creative and express and experience the best parts of yourself? This may be the beginning of another bucket list.

What new things do you want to experience?

Like the IBM commercial says: "You have more power at your fingertips than you could ever have dreamed of." So, what will you choose to do with your power?"

Where can you find inspiration to learn from the "inside out?" Visit Hay House Publishing or Hay House Radio app (research on Google) for great books or programs on enhancing your life. Become a member of the Spiritual Cinema Circle for monthly releases of inspiring short films.

What else can you do to learn from "the inside out?"

How can you be a good role model and messenger as a senior? Perhaps you can start with your own family, friends, neighbors, and colleagues, and then volunteer. Just show who you are. Others will see the authentic you and they will respond, and grow from the experience of associating with you.

Who and what can you mentor?

How can you release stress and relax? Consider breathing exercises (read an introduction to the power of breath later in this book). Begin Yoga or Tai Chi sessions. Start a meditation routine (perhaps go online and join the 21-day mediation program for beginners by Deepak Chopra and Oprah Winfrey).

Write a brief plan for your personal peace below.

Are you grateful? My outlook on life changed dramatically when I started to simply give 'thanks' for my day, every night, as soon as my head hit the pillow. For many years, my nighttime prayers and reflections have included a blessing for every interaction that I have during the day and by feeling gratitude for the privilege of being able to participate in other people's lives.

How can you live in constant gratitude?

Transcend your fears. Step out of your comfort zone. As a senior, you need to avoid giving your precious energy to fear. Instead, look at the world as "come as you are." You need only to focus on blessings and gain joy and peace by helping others. It is OK to try new things, without the old fear. What fears can you transcend?

The question is not whether you can forgive and forget, but only: "Can you forgive?" To become the better version of yourself in this area, it comes down to acknowledging how you are restraining yourself from allowing forgiveness to flow from you. If you cannot forgive or forget, pick one. Make a commitment to forgive or forget (or both). To whom can you offer forgiveness, how…and when?

Your expression of yourself and your spirit is key. The best definition of spirituality that I have heard comes from Neale Donald Walsch: "Spiritualty takes place when you express and experience those parts of yourself that you love the most." Live each day with a high sense of hope, love, joy, gratitude, compassion, and brotherhood. The opportunities to feel your spirit come alive will abound.

How can you best experience and express yourself each day?

Creativity is necessary at all ages but especially for seniors. What sparks your spirit?

Of course, we all have a wide variety of creative skill sets, but I highly suggest that you consider writing a book, perhaps your memoirs. It is an incredible energizing and exciting journey into the depths of your soul. There are many self-publishing outlets like Blurb, Hay House, Smashmouth, The Book Patch, Amazon's Kindle, and more, where you can publish your finished work for under $100, in a bound book or as an e-book. This should be a mandatory project for a senior! Ready to make sparks?

What's your book title? Name some chapters, too.

Your Book Title:

Your Table of Contents:

Introduction:

Chapter 1:

Other Chapters:

What does "Pay it Forward" really mean? How can you choose to 'give back?' Allow yourself to sit in a quiet, peaceful space for an hour. Be genuine in aligning your mind and heart to come up with the best answer to this question for you. List your answers below.

1.

2.

3.

4.

When it comes to staying young,

a mind lift beats a face-lift any day.

~ Marty Buccellla

~ *Chapter 6* ~
There is No Secret Key. You Need to Make the Effort

Like all explorers, we are drawn to discover what's out there
without knowing yet if we have the courage to face it.

~ Pema Chödrön

I found out at a very early stage that there is no miraculous shortcut to expanding one's self-realization. You can simply begin with a small step at a time. Start contemplating with your next thought and just go for it. Once you commit to expanding your awareness in some area of life, you will know what to do and how to be. It comes naturally. Some seniors find they are locked into lifelong habits and behaviors that are difficult to break, even when they know that a change has to occur to allow them more peace, joy, and freedom.

I looked for my personal *secret key* to life for almost two years since the beginning of my spiritual discovery. I had gone through eighteen months of studying spirituality, as offered by my mentor in Kabbalah. Then, one day, I woke up (literally) and recognized that my Kabbalah *glass* was almost full; I was ready to move on, to explore other teachings, more broadly and deeply.

Ultimately, I wanted to find the secret elixir that would unlock the mysteries of life and the universe (really, I felt this way!). Luckily, I was able to carve out one week per month from my role as CEO of a commercial real estate company for my spiritual pursuits, which now became my primary personal quest.

My wife, although very understanding and spiritually enlightened herself, listened to me and acknowledged my passion. However, one day, she was quite surprised, and taken aback, when I arrived home with a box of over 20 books that I had just purchased. I announced to her that, "I am going to my cave [the upstairs den] to begin my quest to discover the *secrets to the purpose of life* from the world's greatest teachers."

During the next six months, I was on an amazing tour of almost every religion, many new age books, audiobooks, spiritual cinema videos, workshops, all types of meditation, yoga, journaling, discussions groups, self-discovery and many, many sessions with gifted, life coaches. I had gone further and further down the rabbit hole in pursuit of universal truth, deeper than I could ever imagine, and still found no single answer. Then, one day, I was blessed with an enlightening discovery, or maybe it was just my time. An exciting *aha!* moment occurred, and finally, I knew that my intense search could rest. It was not the answer that I suspected, though. It was actually a statement of advice, yet it totally resonated with me then and now, and it has been the *wind beneath my wings* ever since.

The *secret* that I learned that one day, while reading in my cave, was revealed to me on one page of a very special book, *The Path to the Higher Self*, written by an American Tibetan Buddhist nun, Pema Chödrön. In her book, Pema wrote this transcendent statement, as if it was destined for me, at that place and time.

If you wish to climb to the tallest mountain so that you can find what you are seeking, know this; that when you arrive at the peak of that mountain, you will only see the foothills of the next mountain to climb, and then the next mountain after that, and on and on.

She was so right! That's what always happened to me. There is no *there*, there. At that point, even though I understood that my "wisdom journey" would never arrive at its anticipated destination, I was not frustrated. My studies were exhilarating and fulfilling. It was just that my goal of finding the secret key was misguided. Thankfully, Sister Chödrön went on to describe the fork in the road that I had just come to:

Rather than to continue up the same path to the peak of the mountain, one should climb back down and find your place, where you can immerse yourself in your daily life, and where you can do the most good. That is where you can find your own beauty and purpose.

"That was the answer that was seeking me," I thought aloud. "Just be the best me wherever and whenever! That's it! OK, I know I can do that, and feel fulfilled." A great feeling and vision of my future suddenly came over me.

My search was validated. I also recognized that I would not have learned this universal truth if I had not done my own *spirituality tour*. I just needed to put in the effort to ultimately learn that the truth that I was looking for was there, as always, right inside of me, as it is right inside each of us. Journey Circle, my spiritually oriented discussion group, was born from this experience.

May I suggest that you choose a new path to explore your own spiritual quest guided by the world's great teachers (yes, I continue to visit them, through books, in my cave), because the wisdom that you seek and discover will blossom inside you. You will soon see the universe, the world, and your own story, for the beauty they are. You will seek and find the many ways to define the better version of yourself and in the process, define your own *call to action*.

Reflections on Success and Significance

Do you consider your life a success?

What are the things that make it so?

Do you consider your life significant now?

What are the things that make it so?

Who are people who have helped you?

Have you acknowledged them?

What are your main gifts, tools, skill sets?

Have you utilized them efficiently?

What are the areas where you did not live up to your potential?

What have you done that is significant for yourself?

What have you done that is significant for your family?

What have you done that is significant for a community?

How can you be significant as a senior?

What things do you need to do to make your senior years fulfilling?

I always wanted to be someone better the next day than I was the day before.

~ Sidney Poitier

~ Chapter 7 ~
Pay it Forward

One thing I know: the only ones among you who will be really happy
are those who have sought and found how to serve.

~ Albert Schweitzer

I pondered the advice of Pema Chödrön for quite some time. It was a call to action for me. Her words, again:

Rather than to continue up the same path to the peak of the mountain, one should climb back down and find your place, where you can immerse yourself in your daily life, and where you can do the most good. That is where you can find your own beauty and purpose.

I knew that I wanted to be a better version of myself, but what might I do on a consistent basis to activate the spirit of her philosophy?

After a good deal of consideration, I thought of the movie "Pay It Forward," and I embraced the concept wholeheartedly. Have you seen the movie? The story is about a young boy who did three good deeds for others in need. In return, all the child asked of them was that they pass on the good deed to three other people, and to ask them to keep the cycle going forward. One good deed might not seem like much, but if everyone did something good for someone else, then the cycle of generosity and kindness could evolve, and humanity would improve itself, exponentially. It is amazing how giving to someone else can make a positive difference, in both lives…*and the ripples flow.*

I think this is a wonderful path for seniors to truly walk the walk of sharing a "good and service" approach to everyone, every day. We can act as a role model and a messenger to influence others to share, and be kind. Acting as a model or messenger is a just another form of paying it forward.

In 2005, I designed a plan to *pay it forward*, in my own way. I formed a discussion group, and named it *Journey Circle.* The primary purpose of Journey Circle was to stimulate my friends and colleagues to join together as a group, to express and experience our own humanity, with open hearts and minds in a supportive way.

A Journey Circle event, to me, represented a treasured time and place to exchange genuine feelings, experiences and helpful resources with caring peers, to support our mutual growth. My vision was that the participants would enhance their personal self-awareness and consciousness and become models and messengers for their own circles of influence. I hoped Journey Circle would become a launching pad for participants to *pay it forward*.

I believe that a form of Journey Circle can benefit today's senior communities. It can become a friendly new gateway to bring people together in neighborhood communities, to listen, express, learn, and support each other. Many of us have spent much of our lives focused on the tribal nature of careers and raising families. In retirement, and when children grow up and move on, it can be difficult to find a place in groups and communities beyond office and home. Starting, or belonging to a Journey Circle group, is a worthy way to forge relationships with peers and share experiences in continued self-growth.

I believe that these types of meetups can be an excellent blueprint for seniors to "mix and mingle" in an enlightening and purposeful way. I have had many requests from people who want information on how to host an event in their home, so I designed a "Journey Circle Event Guide." Perhaps this information will stimulate you to plan an event among your own peers. This guide is presented in Appendix 4 of this book.

Life is not measured by the number of breaths we take,

but by the moments that take our breath away.

~ Maya Angelou

Reflections on How You Pay It Forward

List three ways that you have paid it forward:

1.

2.

3.

List three ways that you can pay it forward, as a senior.

1.

2.

3.

List three ways that others have paid it forward to you, as a senior.

1.

2.

3.

List new ways that you can pay it forward with family and friends.

1.

2.

3.

For what we get, we make a living. From what we give, we make a life.

~ Anonymous

~ Chapter 8 ~
Stepping Out of Your Comfort Zone

You must recognize that you are the producer, director, and actor in the
unfolding story of your life; if you want to change the story,
stretch your mind and your heart.

~ Alan Cohen

We seniors should be encouraged to step out of our comfort zones. Of course, it can be uncomfortable to leave the safety of what you know and step out into the unknown. After all, every time you are about to try something new, the little voice in your head, also known as your ego, begins by whining:

"What are you doing? Stop! Why would you take any risks?"

"What if you look stupid or people laugh at you?"

"What will people think?"

"Who do you think you are? You are not brave /strong /young anymore!"

That is when your alter ego/higher self can come to your rescue. Your alter ego can be a way for you to step out of your comfort zone. It can come to the rescue when you are facing or creating new challenges that may fill you with some doubt or fear. Look at the following:

The ego says: "That's too scary. I better not do that at my age."

The alter ego says: "That sounds exciting! When can I get started?"

The ego says: "But what will they say?"

The alter ego says: "Let them think what they want. Their opinions are not going to get in the way of my living my best life."

The ego says: "What if I fail?"

The alter ego says: "If I fail, at least I will know I gave it a shot."

By switching from your ego to your alter ego, you switch characters and your perspective on life. You will have a window of opportunity during which you can be brave and let go of your hang-ups. Use that window of opportunity to push against your comfort zone and try something new.

As an example, my wife, Marilyn is a born caretaker. She is like her mom, Rose, who was a hospice nurse for thirty years. Just today, as I was working on this book, Marilyn asked if I wanted to join her in driving to Children's Hospital in a nearby town. Our housekeeper, Sandra, has a 10-year-old son, Edwardo, who was diagnosed with a brain tumor that paralyzed a portion of his body. He was confined to a long hospital stay, and his parents and 14-year-old sister visit him for up to 12 hours a day, making time between their work and school schedules, and using the facilities at Ronald McDonald House across the street.

Marilyn surprised me with the short notice request, but I immediately said "yes," although I had to call on Rio to control my ego.

The Rio in me lives in the lesson I learned a few years ago. It is called a *blessed interruption*, and this was a perfect example.

The moment that Marilyn made her request of me, my behavioral instinct let out a little, selfish voice, "No, don't leave, not today, you are on a roll, keep going, let Marilyn make the visit, you can give some money for a gift."

However, Rio is not like my ego. His approach is wiser and compassionate. Rio instantly acknowledged this as a blessed interruption and my inner voice calmly reminded me: "How can you sit and write about the 'better vision of yourself' when you have a real-life opportunity to express and experience your heart and show others you care about their humanity, not just your own?"

Of course, it was a simple decision. We went to the hospital, all of us, Marilyn, Rio and my ego. Of course, once my ego got the message, he took charge, "Ok, we are going to a toy store on the way. We are buying two stuffed animals, crayons and coloring books, a large Spiderman doll, and the game called Simon. It is a great game to stimulate his mind."

Marilyn smiled. She knew "all of me" was on board.

Of course, the blessed interruption was not an interruption at all, but an absolute blessing and an opportunity to *pay it forward* for the many gifts that I'd been given.

The child's family was surprised when we walked in, and happy to see us. We introduced ourselves to Edwardo. His head was severely swollen on one side and only one of his arms could move. He was visibly worn down and afraid. I immediately introduced him to the Spiderman doll as I flexed all of the doll's limbs into funny postures, finally getting a half smile from the brave, young child.

After we entertained him a little longer, I felt comfortable telling him that I'd had polio for four months when I was his age. I explained to him that one side of my throat was paralyzed, but I came out of it, healed, and soon went back to school and played sports, with my friends. I told him that I believed he would do exactly the same as me. He smiled.

What a feeling it was to light up his spirit (and his family's), even for just a short time. Before we left, I took a long, slow walk down from one end of the hospital floor to another. There must have been 25 hospital rooms, hosting kids from four to 15-years-old, in all types of poor health conditions. Many had parents and siblings visiting. To feel the anguish of these families is not possible, unless you are in their position, but a short walk like that certainly raised my awareness, empathy, and gratitude.

And yes, Rio and my ego made sure to thank several of the medical staff for their service.

Now, please share a story of how you have experienced a blessed interruption.

Reflections on Stepping Out of Your Comfort Zone

What was one of the most defining 'out of your comfort zone' moments in your life?

How did it change you?

Reflect on, and write about, a time when you did not step out of your comfort zone, but wish you had:

What are you most afraid of today?

How can you overcome that fear?

What was your most embarrassing moment, and how did you overcome it?

What feels like love to you?

Is it easy for you to express love?

Do you hold back? Why?

How would your friends suggest that you move out of your comfort zone?

If you could change any major event in your life where you were complacent, what would it be and why?

What is something you would normally not do, but want to do?

Get out of your comfort zone. Embrace change. Try something different. It can be something simple like taking a new route home, trying a new food item, try a new fashion, or something bigger like researching a unique field like Artificial Intelligence, or making plans to travel to a new city or country. Let loose and have fun. Laugh more. Learn to tell one good joke. Sing at the top of your lungs. Dance at home. Take a long hike by yourself early in the morning. Commit to a day of sunrise, sunset, and silence (one day of silent self-reflection is a "must do"). Hug everyone you like. Release yourself of your self-imposed boundaries, and be free! You have a choice. Stretch yourself. Make a list of three ways to come out of your comfort zone.

1.

2.

3.

We don't grow older, we grow riper.

~ Picasso

~ Chapter 9 ~
It's About Time

Time is very slow for those who wait. Very fast for those who are scared.
Very long for those who lament. Very short for those who celebrate.
But for those who love, time is eternal.

~ William Shakespeare

At an early point of doing research for *The Senior Season* I decided to reflect on my own experiences within life's big issues, like health, relationships, finances, and faith, and during that process a personal and challenging life issue surfaced. It is a key component of life that strongly impacts seniors, and is rarely discussed.

It is about *time*.

Several years ago, when I was in the midst of exploring life through my relationships with several spiritually oriented people, I met a famous hypnotherapist. She offered me a complimentary consultation in exchange for a favor that I did for her friend. I agreed, and I am so happy that I gave this a chance. The two-hour hypnotherapy and follow-up session with her was quite an experience and it was a revelation to me in many ways. The most interesting thing that came of it was the answer I gave to her primary question when I was under her *spell*.

She asked me what my greatest hurdle in life was, and why.

I responded that "*time* was my greatest challenge. I never seemed *to catch up or have enough of it* to accomplish my goals, trivial or large. The feeling consumed me at times.

Afterwards, as a mentor, she offered me guidance that time is what I make of it.

That's when I learned that I control what I wish to do, when, and how I wish to do it.

Time, as such, is irrelevant if I live in the now, and choose to enjoy life on a moment-by-moment basis. Living in the now allows everything in life to become simpler to deal with, the highs become higher and the lows are lessened, because fear, doubt, and uncertainty are all emotions about the future, not the present.

I can say that when I actively embrace this philosophy, my world does not spin so fast, I am not rushed or pressured. I am calmer and more peaceful. I am more aware of nature. I listen better. I think clearer. I have more empathy, compassion, and a sense of celebrating life.

However, even though I understand this premise, I do not always think and feel in the now. When I do, I can embrace the difference and I can balance my emotions. When I revel in the now, I begin to sit back, reach deeper, and wait for things to develop; I gain a certain perspective, a certain reflectiveness, that I usually was not aware of before.

Time is a big dilemma for many seniors. As you reach the age of retirement, you have more time on your hands than ever before, but you may feel at a loss for how to best use your precious time. For some seniors, there is a tendency to stay busy, just for the sake of it. This *busy-ness* can be a trait; it can be embraced as a stress-laden badge of honor.

For many seniors, instead of finding ways to be busy, it might be wise to lower your focus, and daily stress levels generated by never ending "to do" lists. Instead, center on the present moment, or the now, as Eckhart Tolle discusses in his best-selling book, *The Power of Now,* which I recommend you read.

Here are some of the types of questions the author raises in his book:

How do you relate to the passage of time?

What is worthy of your time?

How can you make every moment matter?

Your answers to these questions can make a huge difference in releasing anxieties about time. They can define how well you live in the present moment, how you age, your level of energy, your sense of fulfillment, and the satisfaction of a life well spent. The acceptance of living in the now can play well within the senior community. Tolle's book offers a new perspective for living in the moment, thereby bringing an entirely new meaning to each day. "When we live in the now," Tolle states, "we can discover an amazing tapestry of things to do, people to see, places to go, and *who* to be, in a very satisfying way, at every moment in time."

It's worthwhile for each of us to contemplate our relationship with time, especially as a senior, when time is perhaps more valuable than ever.

The past is a canceled check, the future a promissory note,

and the present is cash in hand.

~ Anonymous

Reflections on Living in the "Now"

Where are you living right now: the past, future, or present?

Looking inward, how do you relate to the passage of time?

How do you decide what is worthy of your time?

How do you make every moment matter?

~ Chapter 10 ~
Living a Life of Relevance

How can an older person feel relevant?

*It is 100% the person, and 0 % the person's age. Part of what make some
people compelling in their old age is the same thing that made them compelling
when they were young; presence, authenticity, appearance, and some sort of secret sauce.*

~ Anonymous

"Being relevant" has become an interesting topic for me to reflect on and to discuss with my peers. In observing my sense of self in my senior season, I occasionally have flashes of the dynamics of my past social circles and how those groups further attracted others to my everyday life, allowing me to grow, learn, and flourish. I recognize now the paradox facing a senior citizen who has chosen to retire. Our social circles have dwindled dramatically.

I imagine that for most of us, this causes a dramatic shift. Some may feel a sense of disconnection, isolation or loneliness; others may welcome their new circumstances and decide to create a plan for a new lifestyle, one evolving, perhaps, into a high level of contentment.

Sometimes, I catch myself observing my peers as I wonder what they do each day, especially when alone with their thoughts. Do they think about their place on a scale of relevancy past, present, and future? How are they handling the changes? How are they relating to their personal aging process? Are they trying to be young-at-heart or are they just fading into the sunset? Are they happy? Are they content? How has their relevancy changed in regards to their own family, friends, community, and especially, within themselves? Do they even ask these questions?

So, my question to you is: "As you grow older, how can you be relevant in a significant way?" This can be a life altering decision for most Baby Boomers to ponder, yet few of us do.

By definition, "relevance" is inherently tied to some frame of reference, and there is no absolute "true and right" way for determining anyone's individual relevance. You must be the monitor of your own frame of reference.

To most, I believe, relevance is defined as someone or something that is meaningful, connected, and has purpose. It also seems natural that human beings want and need to be relevant. Yet, I am sure that each of us can define personal relevance in vastly different ways, 'relative' to our own perceptions. We all have a different spectrum of relationships with other people and things, with the world at large, and within own minds and hearts. So, how do you identify when, where, how, and with whom you are relevant? How do you figure out how to be your relevant best?

For me, I recognize that my relevance in the business environment, like many retirees, has become negligible since I left my commercial real estate company. I am still active about 10 hours a week in overseeing my own income properties, and I regularly communicate with property managers, tenants, and contractors. I make key financial decisions, but I have a very limited interface with others when compared to my heyday as a CEO, managing a nationwide company with over 100 employees. So, I work to retain relevance by being aware of the challenges of the market and the week's news cycle, which certain of my friends and I discuss and debate, spontaneously. I also stay in touch with several "Young Lions," active entrepreneur friends, who contact me to discuss their latest projects or challenges. In some cases, I mentor them; sometimes I invest with them. I find it stimulating to be "in the game."

I do feel an ongoing sense of relevance with several of my long-time friends, even some from my childhood days. I enjoy sharing in exchanges with past business associates, golf buddies, and many neighbors. With these friends and colleagues, I feel that I am relevant in terms of my contribution to the quality of the ongoing relationships through visits and digital communication, and even sharing some intimate council, now and then.

Recently, my wife and I made a life style shift that has revitalized our approach to this phase of our lives. We moved into Auberge, a wonderful gated community in San Diego, for active seniors, 55 and above. The development is new with resort style amenities, including an attractive clubhouse, pool, Jacuzzi, fitness area, walking trails and more. Importantly, the neighbors who we have been blessed to meet are endearing, and we share a lot of common ground, as friends and neighbors, as we embrace this phase of our lives.

Many retirees across the nation have chosen this type of residential community in order to access a built-in network of peers in their own neighborhood. It has been an excellent decision for most. You are likely to make new friends for life with others who similarly worked hard for many years, raised a family and now are ready to relax and enjoy retirement.

At Auberge, my wife and I are constantly involved in so many activities that it seems like a cruise ship for seniors. It's easy to find people with whom you have much in common and wonderful friendships can blossom. This type of community centric living also provides a welcome opportunity to give back, as neighbors keep an eye on each other, and share feelings of compassion, empathy, and the desire to help. This sense of community creates relevance because of the deep connections that bring people together.

My wife and I also play golf regularly at Fairbanks Country Club, in Rancho Santa Fe. We met on a blind date, on a golf course in 2003, and we have played avidly every year since. We love our golf. We have created many enjoyable relationships with fellow golfers, leading to enjoyable golf dates, dinner parties, and overnight trips. If you can play golf, you will always be relevant; every golfer wants to share their stories! It is an amazing game that can challenge and elevate your mind, body, and spirit on any successful shot, or putt. It's really a virtual walk in nature, especially when errant shots move you off the straight and narrow path.

Family wise, I believe I am more relevant than ever. I feel my input, support, and resources are very meaningful to members of my inner family circle. We each exchange loving sentiments regularly and I have the deepest gratitude and appreciation for being in this position. Of course, my relationship and relevance with each family member is quite different.

My mom, now 94, will live beyond 100, I am certain of it; hopefully healthy and peaceful along the way. It is clear that remaining relevant is an important key to her life force. Fortunately, she has a strong circle of support from family, friends and a daily aide, who keep her active with hearty debates, fun stories, political discussions, and outdoor walks in the neighborhood. I am proud to say that I talk with mom every day, and she can go toe to toe with any current events we discuss!

For my daughters, Tracy and Ashley and my granddaughter Sadie, I feel highly relevant because I stay in touch with their lives and offer my guidance when requested (and sometimes when not requested, too). Throughout the years, I believe that I have and continue to remain one of the most respected male voice in their lives, one which is authentic and genuinely interested in offering unconditional love to make their lives better. This gives my life a precious sense of purpose and meaning.

With my wife Marilyn, I have to say that she makes my life relevant every day. She wakes up with a smile, a cheer, and a bounce in her step; she kisses me good morning and tells me she loves me and *then*…she keeps me on my toes. I am always relevant to her and she makes me know it! She makes me feel younger than I sometimes allow myself to feel and that is a very good thing.

However, with all this said, I believe that my primary issue with 'relevance' is in reference to my relationship within myself. Sometimes, I wonder if I am doing enough, or am I choosing to use my precious time wisely. I wonder what else I can or want to do.

I also acknowledge that I have worked all my life to get to this place and time, but now what? Should I just "take it easy" or should I "get busy doing anything, even trivial things," or do something quite adventurous? Should I choose to delve into a new project with a passion?

Or perhaps I should not care so much. I could just experience and live life, day-by-day, live in the now, and be content. Yet, somehow, something inside of me, says, "You are meant to be relevant. Find that purpose and live it." I agree. I am forever the seeker, I guess. I am OK with that path; it has always been fun. All of these questions have led me to make the decision to write this book, to open gates of reflection on this season, for myself, and others.

For me, it all comes down to knowing that I need and want to feel like I matter. I want to express and experience that I bring meaning, purpose, and enhancement to my life and to the lives of others. I want to feel that each day, I can make a difference, even as trivial as a "butterfly effect," where a butterfly flapping its wings, can cause tiny changes leading to a significant outcome. That's relevance to me, and it can be found everywhere.

Along these lines, another important question to consider is: "How much relevance do you give to your age?" Experts say that not letting your calendar age dictate what you do and how you live is another key to successful aging. Some older adults withdraw from physical activities when they hit certain age milestones, simply because they think they are too old. Or they give up on eating healthy because they think it doesn't matter anymore. I like to focus on wellness, and forget about how old my driver's license says I am. Actually, for my last birthday, I announced that I was celebrating the 16th anniversary of my 55th birthday because it sounds, and feels, so much better to discuss my age in those terms.

I discovered here: http://www.ucl.ac.uk/news/news-articles/1214/171214-feeling-younger-living-longer that researchers at University College of London explored the issue and uncovered a fascinating result: People who thought of themselves as younger actually lived longer! The study included nearly 6,500 men and women with an average age of 66.

Participants were first asked, "How old do you feel you are?" Their replies were:

· 70 percent felt three or more years younger than their actual age

· 25 percent felt close to their actual age

· Five percent felt more than one year older than their actual age

Eight years after being asked that initial question, researchers followed up to determine each participant's status. The first group, which had indicated that they felt younger than their actual age had a lower mortality rate than the other two groups!

So, it just might be true that staying young at heart helps you live a longer life, but it's also wise to be realistic and look at the challenges that seniors face today.

To be relevant means to be the kind of person others depend on, whether for leadership, expertise, acumen, or emotional support.

~ Anonymous

If you can't dance, at least tap your toe.

~ Anonymous

Reflections on Being Relevant

No matter where you are in your senior phase, staying relevant will be a big part of your life style. The biggest barrier for staying relevant is often just feeling like you have a strong sense of purpose. There is no silver bullet to being relevant. You make choices. You make the effort to be engaged. You seek new knowledge. You experiment and take risks. You constantly pursue self-development. Making relevance a priority brings the reward of a retirement lifestyle that can be happy and fulfilling.

Do you have a clear purpose? What is it? What can it become?

List some action items where you can make relevance a priority.

1.

2.

3.

Many family activities, neighborhood get-togethers, hobbies, volunteerism, and interests are inherently social in nature and healthy for body and mind, and a great way of maintaining and expressing a sense of purpose. Living a purposeful life is integral to successful aging. List below some activities to engage in where you feel productive, creative, and social.

1.

2.

3.

Social contacts tend to decrease as you age for a variety of reasons, including retirement, the death of friends and family, or lack of mobility. Without interaction with others, it's easy to limit yourself. You start to think you're too old. Your attitude and enjoyment are influenced by those you are associated with the most so you need to make wise choices in choosing your social circle.

What can you do to broaden and deepen your social circle and mix with people of all ages?

How can you start making a positive shift in your existing relationships?

How can you be more sociable?

You probably have hobbies or interests that you enjoyed when you were younger, but had to put aside when the demands of work and raising a family took over. After you retire, you have the time to enjoy them again or to try new things. As an example, many older people participate in choruses or bands like they did in high school. Others pursue photography, art, writing, crafts, travel, sports, or taking adult education classes. What are your choices? What are your options?

Identify your youthful passions. How can you resurrect some of these activities?

1.

2.

3.

Staying relevant and abreast of changes is challenging, especially with the pace of change today. Your relevance diminishes if you hold on to a past that is not helping your present. You must stay aware of trends; never become a 'has been.' Discover new ideas, pay attention to a broad variety of news, and to what is trending, stay informed, and just keep learning. Don't get into the rut of boring other people by limiting conversation to health troubles, grandchildren, or your latest trip. Keep up (as much as you can) with technology. It is a tool that can put you in the fast lane of relevancy especially if you enjoy online research, newsletters, podcasts, and expressing yourself through blogging. Attend a major conference that is related to your interests at least once a year. (Recently, I enjoyed a three-day cannabis convention in Las Vegas. I learned important aspects of cannabis use for senior medical issues. It was a revelation. Now, I am planning to attend the Consumer Electronics Show (CES), the largest technology conference in the country). You can also look into local chapters of senior associations and register for meet-ups, usually free; these events often include access to educational programs, as well opportunities to meet others and expand your horizons.

How can you stay up-to-date, and what new interests will you pursue or revive?

1.

2.

3.

4.

Some seniors neglect their need to look good because they may not care as much as when they were in the workforce. That's OK, but taking yoga and Tai Chi lessons, buying a new outfit, getting a haircut, taking cooking lessons, and pampering your body with a massage can make anyone feel good about themselves. You should cater to your own needs from time to time to boost your spirit and inner glow. Aging well is essential for physical, mental, and emotional health, and making healthy and happy lifestyle changes can have a positive impact on your life.

How can you enhance your appearance for your own satisfaction?

How can you better take care of yourself?

Is there someone in your family or in your community that you can care for, even for a short visit or on a modest schedule?

Have you ever volunteered? Is this something you can consider? What organizations can you volunteer for?

1.

2.

Do you have a pet? It's a known fact that pet owners remain engaged socially, have less depression, suffer less loneliness, feel more secure, have more motivation for constructive use of time than non-pet owners. Animal companionship facilitates establishing friends, is a social lubricant, gives a reason to get up in the morning, and is an icebreaker. It especially feels good to adopt a rescue dog or cat. Planting or tending a garden can also satisfy your nurturing drive.

What can you do better in this area?

Can you take care of someone or something? Who and what?

~ Chapter 11 ~
Your Inside Bucket List

To have an abundant life, rich and full, means seeing the shortness of the day and seizing it, living the bucket list before the sunsets. It requires the quick gulp and the leaping blind, discarding what is heavy and worthless, investing in eternal things, counting as precious the gifts as they come and holding them loose because they will soon be gone.

~ Catherine L. Morgan

It's time to expand on the work you've done in this book.

The following section offers some intimate questions and general guidelines about how to make choices to become the better version of yourself. Some of the questions will be similar to some that you've already considered, but now, you have a chance to go even deeper.

The notes following each question are presented to stimulate you to create responses that can satisfy your quest. Use this opportunity of self-discovery to create your initial Internal Bucket List, at the end of this chapter.

Your Internal Bucket List

Part One: The Better Version of Yourself

Reflections on Your Internal Bucket List
Part One: The Better Version of Yourself

The primary objective of my Internal Bucket List is to be the best version of myself. My definition of what this means is quite simple: *To express and experience my life in such a way that it will elicit positive change for me and for those around me.*

What does the concept of *"the better version of yourself"* mean to you?

It is good to reflect. To be inspired. To learn. To listen. To share. To become the best that you can become. The following questions and subsequent inspirational statements can spark your path to choose ways to be the best you can be.

Imagine that you are your own advisor from the future. How would you advise yourself to begin to shift your current life style and choices? Write this advice to yourself below:

Can you see yourself as an inspirational role model or messenger? In what ways?

Who can you guide?

How and who can you teach?

What message can you share?

How can you be a better family member?

What can you focus on to improve your family life?

CELEBRATE YOUR GOLDEN YEARS

Make lists of people in your life for each of the following questions:

Who can you forgive?

Who can you apologize to?

Who can you give support to?

Who can you show you care?

Who can you reflect on for wisdom, hope, and dreams?

Regarding friendship, it has been said that, "A friend knows everything about you, but still likes you."
Which of your friends can you say this about? Why?

Who can you share your Internal Bucket List with, if you want to?

Have you genuinely acknowledged your friends?

Who are the five people you spend the most time with, and why?

1.

2.

3.

4.

5.

Who has your back, when you need someone?

Think about your closest, most intimate relationship—the one with a spouse or partner.

Can you improve your relationship by practicing more patience? Giving and earning more love and respect? Being more considerate? Listening better? Communicating more sincerely and clearer? Modifying your personal agenda? Writing love notes? Taking walks together? Getting away with each other and celebrating your life together? Forgiving and forgetting? Hugging each morning? Make each other laugh? How and when will you start on any of these important relationship builders? How can you be a better spouse? Write your thoughts about being a better spouse here:

1.

2.

3.

4.

5.

Parenting is always a challenge, but it has never been as challenging as in today's digital age. This effort requires more than a "seat of the pants" approach. It demands research, study, experiential education, communication skills, compassion, humility, discernment, powerful intention, discipline, and a loving approach? You need to answer the call yourself.

How can you be a better parent?

1.

2.

3.

4.

5.

How can you best guide your child to meet the challenges of the mid part of the 21st century?

1.

2.

3.

4.

5.

What's the state of your relationships with your siblings now? Be honest. *How can you improve on it? Acknowledge your strengths and challenges. How can you stretch each relationship into the light and renew your bonds? How can you be a better sibling?*

1.

2.

3.

The concept of community, and your role in it, is large. Take time to consider who you are and how you fit into the entire landscape of your life.

How can you get more involved and help support your community in better ways? How can you be a better community member?

1.

2.

3.

What are your community's activities and challenges?

1.

2.

3.

How can you acknowledge community members, regardless of their differences?

Have you made an effort to elevate the mood and temperament of your community by being a role model in any way that you can?

Are you compassionate? Do you ask if others need help?

Do you volunteer in a charity group or at a local hospital?

How can you continue to learn and grow your mind and your experiences?

Are you curious?

Personal growth is something that happens even when you're not paying attention to it.

But, it is best to pay attention! *Have you considered your many options, like hobbies, playing musical instruments, engaging in sports and fitness programs? Have you considered writing a poem, a song, a book, your memoirs? Consider your options and interests then write about them here:*

1.

2.

3.

Many seniors continue to learn by attending conferences in different industries like technology, toys, franchise expos, photography, music and more. Perhaps you can join meet-ups groups where you can express yourself in a field that you enjoy.

What choices can you make to be more fulfilled through learning new actions or engaging your creative talents?

1.

2.

3.

One part of you—the soul—doesn't change; the other part of you—your spirit—changes often. Your thoughts, emotions, and feelings factor into your Inside Bucket List in powerful ways—consider the following questions by taking as much time as you need to find your innermost self-wisdom.

What emotional areas can you begin to focus on changing for the better?

1.

2.

3.

You don't need to be better than anyone else; you just need to be better than you used to be. What initial steps can you take to become a better overall you?

1.

2.

3.

You are not stuck where you are, unless you decide to be. Where are you stuck now?

How can you adjust that status?

You cannot always control what goes on outside. But how can you control what goes on inside?

When things are chaotic on the outside, how do you find your peace inwardly?

You get treated in life the way you teach people to treat you. Often, just a smile or a genuine compliment can go a long way. How can you start treating people better?

When the choice is to be right or to be kind, always make the choice that brings peace. Can you do this?

Would you rather be right or be happy? Think about this and write a comment.

Focus on understanding yourself instead of blaming others. Think twice about a situation where you blamed another. Could you have looked at this differently?

Re-focus from what you do not have and take stock in what you do have. Name five quality things that you have that are not material possessions.

1.

2.

3.

4.

5.

Circumstances do not make a man, they reveal him. Think about the many times you have faced adversity and survived, succeeded and/or learned from the experiences. *Write about one of these events.*

Your Internal Bucket List

Part Two: The Choice is Yours

Reflections on Your Inside Bucket List:
Part Two: The Choice is Yours

Write out your traditional bucket list first. List some the things that you want to do and see.

Make an outline of your 'inside' bucket list. These are elements in your life that will allow you to evolve to be the better person that you know you can be, while be fulfilled in the process.

1.

2.

3.

4.

5.

What are the benefits to you if you create and live out an inside bucket list?

What makes you feel happy?

Who brings out the best in you?

What brings out the best in you?

What challenges you?

How will you explore the 'secrets' of your universe?

Where can you best invest your time, talents, and treasure?

Where and with whom can you look for friendship, inspiration, mentorship, and a working model to open up your possibilities and potential?

Notes:

This is my Internal Bucket List

How does it align with your list?

I want to raise my self-awareness. I want to make wiser choices.

I want to have genuine meaning and purpose in my everyday life.

I want to live with joy, peace, happiness, and contentment.

I want to live with love, passion, compassion, and forgiveness.

I want to embrace personal growth, creativity, and positive change.

I want to express my gratitude for my blessings, every day.

I do not want to fade into the sunset.

I want to be active. I want to be more than an observer in the game of life.

I do not want to be busy doing trivial things.

I want to make a difference.

I want to enjoy my time while sharing, helping, guiding, and inspiring others.

I want to pay it forward, by being kind towards others.

I want to engage in rewarding, new experiences.

I want to be the best me that I was meant to be.

I want to always be relevant.

This is Your Inside Bucket List:

Please complete it in your private journal

I want to
I want to
I want to
I want to
I want to
I want to
I do not want to
I want to
I want to
I do not want
I want to
I want to
I want to
I want to
I want to
I want to

The key to your retirement phase is not to give up your job

and just be busy, but to re-gain your heart, and to adjust

the way you view the world and your life.

~ Peter Drucker

~ *Chapter 12* ~
On Death and Dying

Carve your name on hearts, not tombstones. A legacy
is etched into the minds of others and the stories they share about you.

~ Shannon L. Adler

How you die is a profoundly personal journey. I have been comfortable all through my life in believing that death is not a final destination. I do believe in an afterlife, but not in the form of the "me" I am today. I believe intuitively that people have a soul that is part of the cosmic soul that is God. In human terms, I believe that each soul is like a drop of water within the ocean that is God. I do not believe in a heaven or a hell, or a judgmental God. These views have allowed me to have a sense of death as a transformation to a greater destination, one of infinite peace, and joy. I know that many do not believe in God, or feel the same as I do. Most people follow what they were taught or what they learned from others along the way. Still others rely on their intuitive sense, as I do, but they have their own unique perspective, which leads to a wide variety of beliefs. I acknowledge that the truth may be the mystery that eludes us all.

The fact is that our culture does not discuss death because grief is such an overwhelming emotion. We do have a strong tendency to discuss dying, though, since friends, family and associates inevitably fight the fight to stay alive, especially when facing terminal health issues. During these occasions, you are forced to consider the reality and inevitability of your own eventual departure, but you tend to resist discussing any of this with others. Just think, how often in the past few years have you expressed your voice, your feelings, about death itself, and the possibilities of an afterlife? Of course, there are no known answers but it would be good, I believe, for people to accept and express a compassionate view of death and dying so that they can provide support for others and eventually for themselves, during the last phase of one's life.

In recent years, I have given several eulogies, and usually on very short notice. The process of putting my feelings and memories into words that truly honor the deceased is one of deep introspection into the realm of death and beyond. There is a great sense of dual responsibility in acknowledging the deceased properly, and simultaneously comforting their loved ones with a compassionate, loving, and memorable eulogy. As each of us contemplates writing a eulogy, we have to confront and question our own interpretation of death and an afterlife.

In 1999, my grandmother, Nana Rose, passed. I loved her dearly. She remains as one of the greatest human beings I have ever known. I wanted to offer a eulogy that truly honored her, and at the same time, comforted my mom, my daughter and, myself. I researched many eulogies and read extensively on many views of death and afterlife. Finally, I came across one description of death and dying that I have embraced for my own beliefs, and for Nana's eulogy. I share this with others to give comfort in your personal journey. The following excerpt is from the book, *The Prophet*, written by Kahlil Gibran, a world acclaimed American-Lebanese poet.

For what is it to die but to stand naked in the wind and to melt in the sun? And what is it to cease breathing, but to free the breath from restless tides, that it may rise and expand and seek God unencumbered? Only when you drink from the river of silence shall you indeed sing. And when you have reached the mountaintop, then you shall begin to climb. And when the earth shall claim your limbs, then shall you truly dance.

This touches my soul, and I want it read aloud, as part of my family's eulogy to me.

One of my favorite people in life, and a person I can truly say remains as one of my life messengers, and role models, was Stefanie LaRue. Stefanie was misdiagnosed with stage 4 breast cancer at 30 years old. She wore her cancer as a badge of honor. She looked at it courageously, as a powerful opportunity for her to help others, and she did, in a magnificent way. She was a peaceful warrior, she lived with incredible pain and suffering, uncertainty, doubt, and fear, but at the same time she comforted hundreds of other women, who suffered from the same disease. Stefanie engaged in thousands of exchanges on Facebook and arranged one-on-one meetings with survivors, and their loved ones, who visited her from across the country. She offered them her personal experience, advice, and holistic formulas which had allowed her to live for 12 enlightened years, beyond her six-month life expectancy prognosis. I had the honor of being one of her many friends to offer a eulogy on Venice Beach in 2016. Here is my heartfelt eulogy and appreciation for a truly great person, one who brought out the best in me, perhaps it will remind you of a loved one.

At a time like this, our world is shaken.

We have so many questions. We feel so fragile.

Why did this happen? What is the meaning of death and dying?

Stefanie's answer to these questions was simple...Celebrate Life!

So today, let us celebrate the life of Stefanie LaRue, our dear, sweet friend, and a true Earth Angel.

We witnessed Stefanie evolving through a life transformation initiated because of her 12 year battle with stage 4 breast cancer and...I can honestly say that during that time, as a wounded warrior, Stefanie achieved more than almost any person I've ever known.

She went from being a young woman living in shock, pain, and fear to a role model and messenger, inspiring hundreds and even thousands within her cancer community with her beautiful voice, mind, heart, and soul.

Stef recognized that she couldn't change her remaining time on earth but she could change the quality of her life.

She always expressed and experienced herself with authenticity wearing her heart and soul on her sleeve. Stef chose not to live in the shadows or in the darkness.

Instead she chose to walk in the light with her head held high.

She was not a victim of circumstances.

Instead she was a victor of higher consciousness.

She found her purpose in life.

She connected with her spirit.

She served others.

She danced with wolves.

She chose joy.

She made choices to "live organic and live orgasmic."

This holistic life style became her brand to the world.

She looked at life as a great, big art canvas and she threw as much paint on it as she could, creating her own amazing image of the world.

Her love for her friends, her community, and her many rescue dogs was enhanced by her powerful love of life.

Stefanie recognized her purpose in life was to live in her own highest truth.

She fulfilled her destiny.

She truly became the better version of herself.

We will always love you, our precious Stefanie.

I suggest that you set aside a place in your home, with photos or a personally written eulogy, to honor those cherished loved ones who have served as messengers and/or role models, and have passed on. These memories will continue to fill you with the reality, wonder, and beauty of life.

Reflections on Death and Dying

How would you describe the process death and dying to a curious child?

How do you want to be remembered in a eulogy?

Allow yourself to reflect for a moment on the goodness of those people who you cared for, who have passed.

Appendix Section

~ *Appendix 1* ~
The Senior Season: Your Biography

Legacy is not leaving something for people. It is leaving something in people.

~ Peter Strople

You are important. I am important. We are all important. Our descendants deserve to understand who we are, what impactful experiences we have had, and what we can share with them to enhance their lives. This section is a call to action for you, and your family, to create a video biography of your life and times. It can serve as a steppingstone for you to create and preserve a family portrait of memories and memorabilia, for many generations to come.

In 1973, my grandpa Tony passed away. My grandmother, Nana Rose, whom I adored, was heartbroken by his passing.

The week after he passed, Nana Rose asked me to drive her to the cemetery to visit his gravesite. It was a cold, windy, and dark winter's day in New York City. Snow and ice covered most of the cemetery plots and markers. After a long search, we found his tombstone. Nana let out a loud moan and kneeled down on his plot holding onto the stone. It was sad, but very memorable, to see her unconditional love flow passionately before my eyes.

As she knelt at the site for quite some time, I gazed around the cemetery acknowledging the thousands of lives and stories that had passed. As I walked around a bit, I looked at different stones and observed: born 1886, died 1942; and another, born 1899 died 1951, and on and on. "What was the story behind each of these lives," I wondered? "Is anyone still alive who knew them, or at least can recall some parts of their story? Could the answer be 'no?' Of course, that's possible," I thought, as I got a chill from the thought, even more so than the chill from the cold, damp weather.

I looked across the vast array of tombstones and wondered how the life stories of these thousands of souls could have been preserved, for caring and curious descendants. Back in 1973, there were very few venues for sharing family information from one generation to another—besides the old-fashioned way of storytelling and the use of photos, diaries, and an occasional journal. In my reverie, I promised myself that Nana Rose and the rest of my direct family would not be forgotten so easily. Finally, in 1984, I did something about it.

In that year, portable video cameras became available to the public, and I had my *aha!* moment. I wrote out over 100 questions that I wanted to ask Nana Rose about her life story. On Mother's Day that year, I arranged a dinner at my home, where I set up an interview room. I invited my mom to act as the host, and Nana Rose (my mother's mom) was the honored guest, responding to my questions about her life and times, in front of a very hot lamp! After two glasses of Chianti wine for each of them, they finally agreed to do it!

The interview lasted about an hour and it remains a cherished treasure for my mom (now 94), my daughters, grandchild, my wife, and me. In the video, one of the best stories Nana Rose tells is about her first meeting with Grandpa Tony, and immediate elopement when she was only 14, and he was 21 (he was still in the service). Here is an excerpt of the transcript from the video biography, now 34 years later.

My parents were born in Italy. I was the youngest of 11 children. My main chore was to shop for the groceries. One day, I went to the butcher to buy a live chicken (yes, 'live'). As I walked out of the store, the chicken jumped out of my arms and onto the street. Suddenly, I saw a handsome young man, in an army uniform, run towards the chicken and capture it. He then walked towards me and gave me the chicken with a kind, assuring smile and a wink. I smiled back. But then he reached for my other hand and said he wanted to take me on a date. Even though I knew my parents would never allow it, I said 'yes' instantly. He became the first, and last man, that I ever dated; and we stayed married for 53 years, until he passed.

The great thing about Nana Rose telling this story to my mom and me, is that the video shows her facial expressions in a way that takes you back in time, to that wonderful date in 1920, where the 'chicken incident' eventually led to the birth of all the subsequent members of our family! This story was just one of a dozen that Nana Rose shared with us, as she became more and more comfortable relating her life's favorite memories. Nana Rose passed in 1999, but her memory remains for generations to come as her story is now digitized and stored on the iCloud.

I have done similar individual interviews with my mom, dad, and mother-in-law. All of these videos are now family treasures and are stored on the iCloud. My family has already begun filming some videos about my life and times. I am excited to share my stories in a video format for many generations to come.

How about you? Are you ready to be interviewed on video about your life and times? It's your gift to the future. After all, you are one of the first citizens of the 21st century, a pioneer in re-setting your family legacy.

I have created a website (www.theseniorseason.com) on this interview format. It includes guidelines on how to arrange, set up, and create a video biography of a loved one. The site includes over 200 questions to choose from, to customize each interview, and storyline. You can even produce an autobiography by filming an interview of yourself, using your cell phone; or better yet, you and your family can arrange to interview you as a video biography.

The following is a sample from the website:

Your Life and Times

This is an important project for each family

As adults, many of you today don't know much about your own family's origins and history. Society has given way to big changes in time and travel, with little investment in preserving the precious past. Your family experiences, beliefs, and relationships formed your character, yet very few of these personal stories may exist in your family's memory bank, especially as family members die. You have a chance now to change this forgotten journey for yourself and your family. Please take this opportunity to preserve your family legacy.

Just Imagine

Just think if you are honored with a video interview about your life and times. How would you feel? What stories would you tell? What would you like to share and be remembered for? What secrets might you tell? What family traditions to you want carried on? Imagine seeing your own parents, grandparents and even great, great grandparents, in a video interview. How valuable might that be to you and your descendants? Well, perhaps you can be the pioneer in starting this family tradition, now.

By investing just a few hours in a video interview process, describing your life and times, you have a chance to make a permanent record of your valuable experiences, to express your wishes, and to tell *your story* to those who truly care. Your descendants will be able to trace a link to their historical connectors, as they enjoy their ancestors' treasured stories in a powerful way.

This process can also initiate a wonderful tradition, as many family members eventually participate in a multi-generational project, by adding their own stories to the archives. Each video interview can be permanently stored on a wide variety of secure iCloud platforms that offer private code access.

This *family video vault* may enable society to replace cemeteries as the most intimate way to honor a family's history. The personalized and shared vault is a safe and viewable place that can easily store thousands of photos, documents, and hundreds of digital memories, with no special software needed.

The Senior Season Project

The Senior Season website (www.theseniorseason.com) guides family members to create a fun and memorable experience. Enjoy, reflect, and preserve your life and times, in a carefully designed interview format, where you share your valued, intimate, and personal family history. It is a wonderful way to connect families for years to come. The powerful interview questions reveal personal stories that create a refreshing sense of continuity, change, and growth, expressed in the parent's own words, in an interactive, friendly, and memorable way. This amazing experience can be an ongoing family project, scheduled on a holiday or a special occasion.

Choose from Hundreds of Interview Questions:

We suggest that the interviewer and interviewee select (with checkmarks) the questions that will be addressed during the interview, with an asterisk designated for those questions that will be answered in detail. Questions are arranged in a chronological order where possible. Choose questions appropriate for your interview. Add new questions. Create cues to stimulate more questions. Take a look at the questions from the website on the following pages. Enjoy!

Interview Question Guide

Opening narrative by interviewer on video:

Hello, my name is _____.

I have the honor of interviewing _____today.

Today's date is _____.

Also, here today, are _____, _____ , _____.

We all want to be part of this magical interview to show how much we care about _____.

We want _____'s stories preserved forever!

Our hope is that all of our descendants will watch this interview someday and cherish it as the start of a valuable family tradition.

Today, we'll start with early childhood memories.

First, let's ask the "Star of the Show" to introduce him/her self:

_____.

Hello, _____, we want to hear your precious life story.

Ready for the first the first question?

IN THE BEGINNING

- Where and when were you born?

- What were you told about your birth?

- Why were you named _____? Have you picked up any nicknames? When?

- Describe your childhood home and neighborhood.

GRANDPARENTS

- Tell us about any of your grandparents.

- What are their full names?

- What did you call them?

- Where were they born?

- Did they speak other languages?

- How often did you see them?

- Do your parents look like them?

- What's your favorite grandparent story?

- What key words can describe each one of them?

- Who knows the most about their lives, today?

- Do you have any memorabilia representing them?

PARENTS

- Tell us about your parents: include their early backgrounds, home town, and interests.

- Where and when did they meet? Can you tell us the story?

- Tell a fun story about a time you had with dad.

- Now, tell a fun story about you and your mom.

- How are you similar to either of them?

- How are you different?

- What's the best gift a parent gave you?

- What's the best thing that a parent taught you?

- What great family traditions do they want you to carry on?

- What would you say you mom and dad were each best known for?

- Were your parents strict?

- How do you consider yourself as a parent, compared to their approach?

- Was there life purposeful, fulfilling, happy?

- Have you interviewed them about their life and times?

SIBLINGS

- How many siblings do you have?

- What are their names?

- What are their careers and/or passions?

- What's your favorite story about any of them?

- What will you always remember about them? Do they know that?

- If they weren't your relatives, would you be friends?

- Tell us some more about them.

SCHOOL DAYS

- What did you want to be when you grew up?

- When did it change?

- How old were you then?

- Why did you change?

- Any regrets now?

- Tell us something unique that you did (or happened to you) as a child.

- Did you like the schools you attended? Which one did you like best or least?

- Were you a good student? Always?

- What were your favorite subjects?

- Least favorite subjects?

- Were you always healthy?

- Did you ever have a secret hiding place?

- Do you recall any schoolyard fights?

- Do you have any bully stories?

- During high school and college did you participate in school plays or on any teams?

- Did you go to any proms or other school events such as a sports championship game?

- Did you consider yourself a leader? Tell us about your experiences.

- Tell us an unforgettable school story.

- Who was your favorite teacher?

- Did you attend college? Which one?

- What the best lesson that you learn from a teacher?

- What was your major in college? Why did you choose it?

- Would you have changed your major if you knew then what you know now?

- Name one person, besides a teacher, who made a big difference in your school life.

- Did you have a high school sweetheart?

- Did you have a college sweetheart?

- Tell us something unique that you did (or happened to you) as a teenager.

- What was your favorite car, did you buy it?

- Did you ever get into any trouble?

- What did you want to become in the future when you were a teenager?

- Did you get into trouble at school? Why?

YOUR FAVORITES

- What's your favorite thing that you ever did as a child? As an adult? Why?

- What was your favorite vacation anywhere?

- Which countries have you traveled to? Which is your favorite? Why?

- Do you like traveling? Why?

- What's your favorite fun place to go?

- Tell us about your favorite home?

- What has been your favorite hobby throughout your life? Why? When did you begin?

- Are you still active with it? What do you want to accomplish? Was it about joy? Success? Passion? Accomplishment?

- What other hobbies have you (do you) enjoy? Why?

- Any advice for others pursuing these hobbies?

- Do you like movies, games, reading?

- What are your favorite movie, game, book?

- Do you have a favorite sport? Why?

- Who are your favorite teams?

- Who are your favorite actors? Why?

- What's your favorite movie? Why?

- What's been your favorite TV show?

- Who are your favorite singers? Why?

- Have you ever played any instruments well? Can you sing?

- Who have been your best friends throughout your life?

- What have you enjoyed doing together, as friends?

- Who is your favorite hero or role model?

- Do you have a favorite joke or story?

- Do you like to cook?

- What's your favorite food to cook? To eat?

- Do you dream a lot? Tell us a story about your experiences with sleep.

- Have you ever kept a big secret? Can you tell us now?

- Tell us about your favorite pet?

- What are your favorite animals?

- Have you ever fed, or ridden a farm animal?

- If you invited your favorite famous persons to dinner, who would they be?

- Besides us, who are your favorite relatives? Why?

FAITH and RELIGION

- What was your faith as a child? How did you participate in your faith then?

- Have you changed your beliefs? Why?

- Do you like going to services?

- How do you feel other religions?

- Do you believe in God?

- Do you talk with God? Do you pray daily?

- Does God answer you?

- Do you believe in heaven or hell?

- Do you believe in angels and miracles?

- Do you believe in life after death?

- What can you tell me if I want to learn not to be afraid of anything?

- What does being good mean to you?

- What is your opinion and experience of evil in life?

HOLIDAYS

- What is your favorite holiday? Why?

- Do you get together often with relatives?

- What traditions do you have each year? What makes it special?

- How have you celebrated your birthdays? What was your favorite?

- Do you like parties?

- Do you like surprises?

- What is the best gift you ever received?

- What's the best gift you ever gave?

MEMORIES

- What's your first memory in life?

- What's the most important thing that has happened to you in your life?

- What have been some of the most exciting things in your life?

- What's the biggest world event that happened in your lifetime?

- What's the hardest thing you've ever done?

- What is the best thing you have ever done?

- What do you think the next part of your life will be like?

- What are your best lessons learned?

- When you look at yourself in the mirror, what is the first thing that you look at now?

- Tell us your favorite things to ponder as an adult.

- What did you wish you did but never did?

- What do you want people to know about you?

- Where would you live if you had no family, no boundaries, and incredible riches?

- Have you helped people way beyond their expectations?

- Have you mentored anyone?

- What's the best thing that you ever created (beyond your children)?

- What's are some of your greatest sports successes?

- What's your greatest non-sports, non-business, non-family success?

- What would your life be like if you only did things that you like and never did things you didn't like?

MORE ABOUT YOU

- What are your thoughts about money?

- Are you a spender or a saver?

- What would you do with $1,000,000, if you had to spend it in a week?

- What do you still want to learn?

- What superhero are you like?

- What's your worst mistake in life?

- What things have you tried to learn and couldn't?

- What's your biggest fear?

- What fears have you overcome?

- Have you ever been interviewed on TV?

- Has a photo of you appeared in a publication?

- Who are the most famous people you have ever spoken with?

- What does courage mean to you?

LOVE and MARRIAGE

- When you were a teenager, how old did you think you would be when you married?

- How many children did you expect to have? Boys? Girls?

- Where and when did you meet your spouse?

- Was it love at first sight? Tell us about your first meeting and first date.

- What did you see in each other? What did you feel about each other?

- Did you know you would marry right away?

- How long was it before you married?

- Where and when did you marry?

- Who was your best man/maid of honor?

- Do you have the photos of the wedding?

- Did all the parents approve?

- Where did you first live?

- Where did you honeymoon?

- What was your newlywed life like?

- How were you earning income?

- Were you comfortable?

- Any unique stories to share about the early stages of your marriage?

- Please tell us more about your marriage(s).

- Do you have any comments about love, partnership, marriage to share?

PARENTING

- If you had unlimited money today and you were only allowed to spend it on your children what would you do?

- What is one thing you would choose to do differently with or for your children?

- What's the best and worst things about the times when you were first a parent?

- What's the best and worst things about being a parent today?

- How did you differ from your own parents' approaches to parenting?

- How would you want your children to differ from your approach?

- As a parent, what are your concerns about being "politically correct?"

- How do you see cyber bullying, alcohol, and drugs?

- As a parent, are you OK if your state approves the legalization of cannabis?

- Where have you traveled with your children? Where do you wish you had gone?

- What are some of the favorite thing that you did with your kids?

- Do you have grandchildren? Tell us about them?

- Do you have other comments about your experience as a parent or grandparent?

CAREER

- How many careers, or businesses, have you had? Please describe them.

- What was your first job?

- What is your most recent job?

- What's been your favorite pursuit with economic benefits? Why?

- What was your least favorite position? What happened to change it?

- If you wished for a career do-over, what pursuit would you have followed instead?

- What are your primary accomplishments? What are you especially proud of?

- Have you ever earned any awards, promotions, or publicity (positive or negative)?

- Have you ever created or built anything?

- Have you had anything published?

- Who is the most famous business person that you ever met?

- Who has been your role model be?

- What have you learned about money over the course of your life?

- What have you learned about success? Teamwork? Failure? Retirement?

- What have you learned about people management, being a boss, fairness, regulations?

BUCKET LIST

- OK, here's your chance to express your Bucket List, inside and out!

- Do you have a Bucket List, now? Can you update it?

- What travel plans do you have on your bucket list?

- Hobby plans?

- At home plans?

- Relocation plans?

- Charitable and community plans?

- Spiritual plans?

- Family plans?

- Friendship plans?

- Financial plans?

- Are you writing a book?

- Are you writing your memoirs?

- What are your health and fitness plans?

- Retirement plans?

- Do you have an internal bucket list? This is a list of how and what you want to do and feel to have greater meaning, purpose and fulfillment, in your life.

MILITARY

- Did you ever have a desire to be in the military?

- Did you enlist? When? Why? Where were you deployed? How long?

- Tell us some of your interesting stories of basic training, or being stationed overseas.

- Tell us your favorite stories.

- If you could do it over, would you? Why?

- Do you stay in touch with others you met during your enlistment or career?

THE FUTURE

- Are you excited about being a senior? Why?

- What do you think that you'll do in full retirement?

- Do you have hobbies you want to start or pursue?

- If you could have any job in the world going forward, what would that be?

- During the next year, what are you looking towards the most?

- Would you like to comment about politics…past, present, future?

- How many grandchildren do you think you will have?

- What excites you about the world for the future? Can you tell us why?

- Do you believe that we will find life elsewhere in the universe?

- Do you believe that aliens will be found or will visit Earth?

- Will there be a World War III?

- Will terrorism stop?

- Will all cars be driver-less?

- Will private citizens be able to fly to and land on the moon?

- Will we own a functional robot, as if they were best friends?

CONCLUSION

Please give us some concluding remarks by summing up your life experience and leaving a message for us, and your future family members.

Who would you like to interview next, in your family?

Notes: Add additional appropriate questions here:

From Roots to Leaves: My Best Tips for Tending Your Family's Tree

You already are a part of one—a leaf! The key to understanding the depth and breadth of your family tree is the attention you give to it. Seniors have more time now than perhaps ever in their lives to spend discovering their origins and understanding their place on the tree. Because history has gone on for so long, it can be intimidating to find a place to begin.

The roots of every family's tree are deep, and it is nearly impossible for a beginner to start at the roots. It's best to begin on the branch where you are now and work your way back in time. Once you start, you'll find that the project can be exciting. You'll want to keep gaining new insights about the reason you came into being!

Here are 10 tips that I found useful while pursuing my family's personal history:

1. Begin with a format, a chart you can fill in with your name, the names of your immediate ancestors and current family members. A great place to start is with the National Archives. Download free recordkeeping charts here: www.archives.gov/files/research/genealogy/charts-forms/ancestral-chart.pdf

2. Once you've completed this homework assignment, you're ready to start collecting stories. Ask your oldest living relatives if they'd be willing to assist you in adding new birth/immigration/health/career information to the names you've already collected. Then ask them if their own knowledge goes back further than yours.

3. Clear some space on your desk to prepare room for gathering any historical documents your family members saved. Birth and death certificates, military records, photo albums, packets of letters, scrapbooks, memorabilia boxes. Consider these as treasures, and make a good plan to store them after you and others have seen their value to your family. Learn about archival preservation of family papers and photographs here: www.archives.gov/preservation/family-archives.

4. At this point, it's a good idea to educate yourself about the wealth of materials available on the internet to those who are searching for personal past history. Websites such as www.ancestory.com and www.findmypast.com are great places to begin. You'll be allowed access to free information to a point; be prepared to pay a small fee in exchange for the services they offer beyond what gets you started.

5. Now that you are in the realm of information that died with your ancestors, you need to rely on written records kept by institutions and entities that had contact with your relatives long ago. You can do your own research with the U.S. Census Bureau, immigration records such as those held at Ellis Island in New York, military service records, newspaper archives, birth and death certificates kept and held by regional government institutions. If you've paid a membership fee to use a genealogy website, you can do a lot of this research all in one place.

6. By the time you get to this tip, you'll realize how much time and thought you've invested in this project. Take some time to write about what you've discovered on a personal level—after all, you are the one who is creating your own role as an ancestor. Why do you think it was important for you to learn your family history? Why do you think it is important for your family members to care about it as much as you do? You may want to write a letter and leave it for future generations to discover, or, create some type of time capsule to be appreciated by those who'll still be aware of you and your life 100 or more years after you've passed into the realms beyond Earth.

7. All family histories contain elements of good and evil. As you discover each, hold no judgment in your heart. Feel only love and appreciation for lives well lived in health, abundance, grace and ease, and for the lives filled with struggle, sorrows, illnesses, punishments. Ask yourself if you see any patterns in behavior. How are these patterns relevant to you and your family members today?

8. Share! You are bound to get a reputation as a record-keeper for the work you've done on your family's personal history. As much as you might feel unappreciated by others in your family who do not hold an interest in the past, open your heart and still share what you've discovered with them.

9. Working with the past can be isolating, so when you feel alone in both the work and joy of discovery, seek out others who are taking the time to do similar work. Your local library is a great place to find a community of seekers; there are many places on the internet where you may communicate with others who are doing research and answering questions based on the expertise they've accumulated.

10. If you become interested in the nature of time itself while researching the history that was contributed to Earth by your relatives, I highly recommend reading a little book written by a theoretical physicist who is able to make the concept of time very clear. Carlo Rovelli published The Order of Time in 2018, and I believe that this book itself will become a classic.

~ *Appendix 2* ~
Wellness: Just Breathe, Just Be

The mind and the breath are the king and queen of human consciousness.

~ Leonard Orr, a pioneer in the process of rebirthing

Throughout this book, I've addressed *spiritual* health. There's another aspect of health that can help you a great deal, yet is taken for granted by many. It is the power of the breath and it has fascinated me for many years. It is a key component of wellness.

On my personal bucket list, first written in 2006, I was hoping to embark on a one-year excursion around the world (as a retired senior) to learn all about Eastern breathing exercises known to heal and enhance life on a physical, emotional, intellectual, and spiritual basis.

My objective was to enjoy a broad social and cultural exposure, while doing experiential research for the project. I planned to meet and interview many of the leaders in the field to participate in a wide range of programs, master dozens of exercises, and techniques and then be able to share the information with a wide audience. I envisioned producing a documentary film on the subject of breathwork, with a guidebook titled, *A Worldwide Breath Enhancement Guide*, to demonstrate the benefits of conscious breathing to mainstream society.

I did not go on this trip. Let's just say that *life* got in the way. However, I did invest quite a bit of time and effort in researching the field and I want to share a some of this information with you, including, in the next appendix, a list of internet resources for meditations and breathing apps, that can quickly deliver wonderful exercises, demonstrating the power of breath, right at the tip of your nose.

In the study of breath, you immediately realize that its power can help your life in many ways. Breath is the wonder of life. It is your greatest gift.

From your first breath, when you sucked in oxygen, you learned that the act of breathing was the key to your life force. Your breath—through your esophagus, diaphragm, lungs, capillaries, and blood cells—powers every thought, word, and muscle movement you think, say, or perform. Every system of your body depends on it for energy. The bottom line is that breath is the fuel for your life engine and your entire being: physical, emotional, intellectual, and spiritual.

Yet, you and everyone else, usually takes breath for granted. Diaphragmatic or belly breathing is the most efficient form of breathing (like what a baby does), yet, over 80 percent of all people worldwide do not breathe properly, and do not even understand why. Conscious breathing (when you control your breathing) techniques are well known around the world, but practiced by relatively few people. You can learn a wide variety of simple exercises allow you to control your breath in ways that harness its power to create positive energy and healing.

The human body takes about 20,000 breaths a day; imagine the difference in your health if you enhance your breath's power by just five percent each day. The simple truth is that when you breathe better, you feel better.

I believe everyone needs to have a new awareness that the quality of breath impacts the quality of life and it is another way to activate the better version of yourself.

There are literally hundreds of video breathing exercises that you can access on You Tube. I recommend reviewing the most popular, noting the number of visitors.

My favorite breathing exercise is one that I learned from the website of Andrew Weil, M.D. This technique is called the "4-7-8 Relaxing Breath Exercise" and it is as simple as its name implies. It can be used multiple times each day, for moments at a time, in an inconspicuous way. One can use it for relaxation, sports performance, speaking, and personal communication—even before sleep. It stimulates you to relax by releasing tension and anxiety through a breathing pattern that is slow, quiet, deep, and circular. I have used this technique for several years now, and have found it an easy tool to relax and reset myself. I use it across so many aspects of my life—from moments before making a presentation, to just before bedtime, and even as part of my preparation before an important golf shot. It works!

I suggest that you visit Dr. Weil's website (www.drweil.com) for the full details of this powerful, conscious breathing exercise, plus more of his valued insight on enhancing the power of your breath.

Meditation

Meditation is another aspect of breathing practice that is a powerful tool for seniors. Meditation is the art of relaxing the mind, using attention to your breath, so that you may increase your clarity, relax your mind and heart, and, experience inner peace. It is not hard to learn to meditate and when you feel its benefits, it can become a lifelong practice. Ten to 15 minutes a day is all that you need to do.

Meditation is a fascinating, yet simple way to enhance your life. I have practiced it on and off for many years, and never sustained the practice, always allowing the choice of "busyness" to prevail in my every day consciousness, thereby creating inconsistency. But when I do feel overwhelmed, stressed out, or just need some genuine "me" time, I practice meditation for a few days, and it's always wonderful. It took me about five sessions to realize that it's not some flakey, new age "thing." It is a gentle, peaceful, and yet powerful practice. It's is a great way to go through life. You just need to have the discipline to care enough.

If you have never meditated, I suggest that an excellent gateway is through the 21-day meditation experience series (there are several focus choices in the series) presented by Oprah Winfrey and Deepak Chopra, available through Amazon or the Chopra Center. It's amazing! Visit this website for more details on the program: www.Oprah.com/meditation

Breathwork and Rebirthing

Breathwork is another aspect of breathing exercise and one that I have explored deeply. It is also known as known as "rebirthing." Very few people know about this breathing modality and I have practiced it for more sessions than any students I know. My enlightening experiences were life altering because of the fact that I had several "out of body experiences" where I felt I was in a true altered state—and it was simply because of my breathing pattern. My breath facilitator and mentor, Christiane Schull, is an incredibly gifted and amazing person. We met in 2005 for my first introduction to breathwork. After one session, I immediately signed up for twelve more sessions, once a week for three months.

A 'session' usually last about two hours. The breather sits and talks with the facilitator during the first hour on any topics of personal concern. The second hour begins the breathing process. The breather lies down, with the facilitator seated beside them, and then the facilitator initiates the breathing pattern to be imitated by the breather. The breathing is full, deep, and circular (no pauses), with whoosh sounds, as you inhale and exhale, as you establish a consistent tempo. You breathe in this way for about an hour.

As difficult as that may sound, time flies by because you enter an altered state of consciousness as you relax into the conscious breathing pattern. Slowly, it seems like your mind, body and spirit become one, in awareness, as your body takes in more oxygen than usual and changes the carbon dioxide (CO_2) level in your brain. At this point, your altered state of consciousness can lead to many paths via the power of your mind to visualize. I had different experiences in each session—no two were similar in what I saw and how I felt. The experience was unique, memorable, and powerful.

This is a truly remarkable experience that I highly recommend. To participate, you can look online for a rebirthing facilitator near you and then schedule a free consultation. In short: Just Breathe, Just be!

~ *Appendix 3* ~
Breathwork and Meditation Resources

1. Article about breathing and its impact on meditation:

http://www.doctor-recommended-stress-relief.com/Abdominal-Breathing.html

2. Harvard Health offers information on how to learn diaphragmatic breathing:

www.health.harvard.edu/lung-health-and-disease/learning-diaphragmatic-breathing

3. Three breathing exercises are offered by Andrew Weil, M.D.:

www.drweil.com/health-wellness/body-mind-spirit/stress-anxiety/breathing-three-exercises/

4. This website offers "Relaxation Exercises" at:

www.patient.info/health/anxiety/features/relaxation-exercises

5. "Yoga Breathing to Fall Asleep Fast," article by Heidi Kristoffer:

http://www.shape.com/blogs/working-it-out/yoga-breathing-fall-asleep-fast

6. "Breathing Exercises – Using Deep Breathing Can Decrease Stress, Help Lower Blood Pressure and Reduce Neck and Back Pain," article:

http://www.necksolutions.com/breathing-exercises.html

7. Golfers…this one's for you: "Breathe your way to better posture," by Roger Fredericks:

http://webcache.googleusercontent.com/search?q=cache:http://www.golf.com/instruction/br eat he-your-way-better-posture

8. "The Optimal Breathing Self Mastery Kit" by Michael White. This is an excellent web site for everything you want to know about the power of breath, including a breathing test:

www.breathing.com

9. Stanislav Grof is a pioneer of breathwork; for background and information visit this site:

www.holotropic.com

MEDITATION

1. An article by Jack McCoy titled, "Meditation Breathing Techniques" is found here:

http://www.project-meditation.org/htm/meditation_breathing_techniques.html

2. Read an article titled, "Breathing Techniques" here:

http://www.clear-mind-meditation-techniques.com/breathing-techniques.html

3. The New York Times Meditation newsletter offers a list of articles to peruse:

www.nytimes.com/topic/subject/meditation

4. Offerings of "Meditations that Heal" on YouTube:

www.youtube.com/user/PositiveMagazine/featured

5. A good blog centered on meditation topics:

www.aboutmeditation.com/blog/

6. See "Sample Relaxation Exercises" on this website:

http://sleepfoundation.org/insomnia/diagnoses-treatments/relaxation-exercise/

And remember: Life is too short to drink bad wine.

~ Johann Wolfgang von Goethe

~ *Appendix 4* ~
The Journey Circle Guide™

In 2005, I designed a plan to *pay it forward*, in my own way. I formed a discussion group, and named it "Journey Circle." The primary purpose of Journey Circle was to gather 15-20 friends and colleagues to join an informal, invitation only, discussion group, so that we could express and experience our own humanity, with open hearts and minds, in a supportive way. Each meet-up explored a topic on a meaningful aspect of life, chosen by the host, or facilitator.

These Journey Circle events represented a treasured time and place to exchange genuine feelings, experiences and resources with caring peers, to support mutual growth. My vision was that the participants would enhance their personal self-awareness and consciousness and become models and messengers for their own circles of influence. I hoped Journey Circle would become a launching pad for participants to *pay it forward*, through a greater sense of awareness and compassion.

I believe that a form of Journey Circle can benefit today's senior communities. It can become a friendly new gateway to bring people together in neighborhood communities, to listen, express, learn, and support each other. Many of us have spent much of our lives focused on the tribal nature of careers and raising families. In retirement, and when children grow up and move on, it can be difficult to find a place in groups and communities beyond office and home. Starting, or belonging to a Journey Circle group, is a worthy way to forge relationships with peers and share experiences in continued self-growth.

I have had many requests from people who want information on how to host a Journey Circle event in their home for family, friends, or neighbors. I believe it can be an excellent blueprint for seniors to mix and mingle in an enlightening and purposeful way.

Journey Circle's stated mission is to enhance everyone's life journey through the celebration of spiritual, religious, cultural, and social diversity. It is all about celebrating life by listening, learning, expressing, and experiencing yourself with like-minded guests in an open, informal roundtable discussion group. It's engaging, it's memorable, it can be life altering, and it's fun!

The following is the intent of Journey Circle meet ups. I included this message as part of the invitation, it sets the tone for guest' expectations.

We are reminded, before we begin the event, that we are inspired by the concept that life is a journey and each of us determines which path we will take.

Journey Circle is a gathering of seniors who care; all good and well intentioned.

Many come from different cultures and traditions.

They cherish their paths and respect each other's.

It is a quest for wisdom, peace and happiness which calls them together.

Journey Circle, fits none of the traditions and yet all of them.

There is an unspoken proverb sensed by those on this Journey:

One light, many lamps. One journey, many paths."

Each participant serves as a lamp, bringing his or her own principles, perspectives, and practices to open the door to the world of goodness, gratitude, and service,...to see the vision of the better version of self, individually and collectively.

We come together as students and as teachers...as brothers and sisters, in a spiritual family.

And, in the service of this great purpose, we meet in friendly discussion to compare and contrast, to test, and to share with each another, in free and open discussion.

Our goal is that our participants are blessed with an aha! moment that will last a lifetime. When this happens, then we all participate in a powerful event and a great deed.

Discussion Topics

Topics for each event are diverse. Here is a short list of topic samples for seniors:

Life's purpose

Compassion

Forgiveness

Happiness

Passion

Unconditional love

Life as a peaceful warrior

Relationships

Relevance

Paying it forward

Finding the Light

Parenting

Living in community

Wellness

Overcoming fear

Caretaking of others during illness, dying, and death

A Traditional Bucket List

An Inside Bucket List

The Journey Circle is Meant to Be Friendly, Informative and Reflective

Journey Circle does not subscribe to any theology, dogma, or set of rules. There are no rituals. There is nothing to belong to. There are no books, no gurus, and no underlying belief systems, no fees. It is certainly not a secret club, church, or ministry, a dogmatic religious or spiritual, "my way is the best" type of forum that divides and excludes rather than joins and includes. We meet in friendly discussion to compare and contrast, to test, and to share with each another, in free and open inquiry.

The Simple Objective of Journey Circle

The ultimate hope is that Journey Circle will empower a number of its participants to experience an *aha!* moment—a moment of awareness, a dramatic and empowering change in one's attitude or perceptions towards life, a seeing with different eyes, a moment of personal truth revealed.

Guests understand that even if only one of the participants embraces an *aha!* moment, in their mind or in their heart, then all will have participated in a great and noble deed. This is the "wind beneath the wings" of the Journey Circle.

The Role of Each Participant

- Leave your mask at the door, when you arrive

- Listen with an open mind

- Express yourself with an open heart

- Respect all other guests

- Make a pledge to maintain confidentiality of the event's intimate discussions

- Remember that the event is not about the topics themselves…it's about all of the guests and how they relate within the flow of the discussion

The Role of the Host or Facilitator

The role of the host and/or facilitators is to have the guests understand and participate freely in the evening's format, and to guide the discussion in an empowering manner. Simply put, the facilitator's objective should be to create a "comfortable place" where participants "can be themselves."

Guest List and Invitations

Generally, a guest list of 15 to 20 people will lead to an event participation of 12 to 15 guests. It's important to identify people who would be genuine in their approach to the event, and especially to the topic, and to other guests; people who can offer sage experience and have the capacity to listen, learn, and contribute. After the initial event, the guest list tends to expand as guests typically want to introduce new members to the group.

Pre-Event

After guests return their RSVPs and the participants are determined, I advise the host to do online research on the topic, and forward pertinent reference material to the rsvp list, to stimulate the depth of the discussion, during the event. This proactive process was very effective for my groups, throughout more than 25 events.

The Social Phase of the Journey Circle

The evening begins as a social reception. During the first hour, guests can relax and get to know each other in a friendly and comfortable manner. Beverages and snacks can be made available. This social gateway helps develop a level of relaxed personal connections and sets the tone for an open and friendly discussion to follow.

The Circle

After the social reception, guests are invited to sit in a circle of chairs. The circle is the most ancient symbol of connection. It denotes the equality among all participants and their respect for each other. The "center" of the circle soon becomes filled with contributions and narratives from each guest, eventually forming a vortex of experiential information, coming alive in the mind and heart of each guest, re-creating their own perceptions.

The Beginning of the Discussion

The host/facilitator begins the main phase of the event by introducing Journey Circle's simple objective. He then outlines the evening's format, the topic, the timetable, and a brief description of the discussion process for the event. Occasionally, a guest may be invited to begin this part of the evening with a special reflection of an *aha!* moment or a personal story revealed at a recent Journey Circle event, to spark the evening's discussion.

The host then begins the discussion format by asking each guest to identify themselves and to read an inspirational topic card placed below their seat (which pertains to the topic and creates conversational stimulus). After this full round of brief guest introductions, the host invites a volunteer guest to offer their input or personal experience on the subject matter. The guest then selects the next contributor (if there are no volunteers the discussion evolves under the guidance of the host). The discussion circulates around the room in a random manner, and moves in many different directions, around and into, the heart of the subject matter.

The Parting Phase of the evening

At the end of the event (typically three hours) a bell is tolled and participants are encouraged to take a break before coming back in the circle for the closing phase of the evening, when members can volunteer to summarize and express what they learned and experienced, and reveal the surprising connections they made.

At the host's option, there may be a special music selection played 'live' to complete the evening on an upbeat and/or especially meaningful note. Coffee, tea, and dessert may follow, allowing guests to mingle before leaving.

The Journey Circle format is adaptable. Here are some other versions of the event:

> *One Event Speaker:* A speaker can make a stimulating presentation on the featured topic. The Journey Circle format can then be initiated for the balance of the evening, with the speaker and host as the facilitators of the discussion group.

> *Discovery Circles*: This roundtable format is actually a mini Journey Circle. It allows four to six guests to break into smaller groups and interact with multiple guests and topics, changing tables and topics three times in one hour segments) during the same evening, or perhaps acting as a facilitator at one of the tables. Each circle's topic is

similar to those offered in Journey Circle events but are more intimate, personal, and self-revelatory because of the small, open format that allows for animated debate and discussion. These Discovery Circles are typically oriented and facilitated by someone who is very knowledgeable in the field and/or speaking from personal experience about a challenge or discovery. They invite members of the circle to share experiences for their mutual benefit.

~ *Appendix 5* ~
Recommended Browsing for the Savvy Seniors

While some of the children and all of the grandchildren of the Baby Boom generation members are natives to technology, many of those over the age of 55 in 2018 are not…and that is unfortunate. The internet is the biggest social innovation since the automobile, and it offers just about as much freedom to travel the lands of cyberspace as your car has the freedom to go where you drive it. Here are some great sites for seniors. Take the ride!

AGING

AARP: aarp.org

Love to Know Seniors: seniors.lovetoknow.com

Sixty and Me http://sixtyandme.com/start/

Retirement Life Matters: retirementlifematters.com

Considerable: www.considerable.com/welcome-considerable/

DATING AND SOCIALIZING

Senior Match: www.seniormatch.com

Dating for Seniors: www.datingforseniors.com

Seniors Only: SENIORSonly.club

Senior Forums: Seniorforums.com

DISCOUNTS

Groupon: Groupon.com

The Senior List: www.theseniorlist.com/biggest-list-of-senior-discounts/

CAREGIVING

Assisted Living Directory: assisted-living-directory.com

Family Caregiver Alliance: www.caregiver.org/caregiving

EMPLOYMENT

Work Force 50: workforce50.com

GRANDPARENTING

Websites for grandparents: http://www.grandmagazine.com/2015/08/11-best-websites-for-grandparents-holding-page/

HEALTH

Web MD: webmd.com

The Mayo Clinic: mayoclinic.com

National Institutes of Health Senior Health: nihseniorhealth.gov

Medicare: medicare.gov

HUMOR

Suddenly Senior: suddenlysenior.com

Swap Meet Dave: swapmeetdave.com

ONLINE GAMES

www.onlinegameforseniors.com

PERSONAL FINANCE

Investopedia: Investopedia.com

The Money Alert: themoneyalert.com

Consumer Reports: consumerreports.org

TECHNOLOGY

Age in Place Technology Watch: ageinplacetech.com

Internet Games for Seniors: http://guideforseniors.com/blog/senior-online-games/

The Senior's Guide to Computers: seniorsguidetocomputers.com

TRAVEL

Road Scholar: roadscholar.org

Evergreen Club: evergreenclub.com

VOLUNTEERISM

Go Overseas: www.gooverseas.com/volunteer-abroad/senior-travelers

Retired Brains: www.retiredbrains.com/volunteer.html

The Senior Season

About the Author

A member of the Baby Boom generation, Robert Robotti was born in 1946 and raised in New York City. Residing in Southern California since 1985, Robert and his wife Marilyn enjoy strong family ties, great friendships, and golf.

Robert is a serial entrepreneur. He founded two enterprises and grew them to success during a career span of over thirty years. His International Export Company was headquartered in New York's World Trade Center. After relocating to Los Angeles, he founded a commercial real estate investment firm that acquired and managed over 120 commercial assets, nationwide.

Curiosity inspired Robert to write *The Senior Season*. He sought to identify a 'secret sauce' that would make his transition to quasi-retirement filled with purpose, meaning, fun, and fulfillment. He realized that while many of his peers lived an active lifestyle, and wielded significant influence over the quality of their lives, they weren't able to express a clear personal plan to make the most of their golden years. They were unsure of their many options.

An 'inside bucket list' is Robert's answer to focus on feeling good about who he is and how he feels rather than what he wants to do or see. Readers of *The Senior Season* are offered interactive tools to accomplish this type of a lifestyle plan—and find the keys to open doors of reflection, revival, and relevance.

Made in the USA
San Bernardino, CA
20 September 2018